A DEEP BUT
DAZZLING
DARKNESS

Exploring God's "Dark Side"
in the Light of His Love

A DEEP BUT DAZZLING DARKNESS

Exploring God's "Dark Side" in the Light of His Love

BY

JENNIFER JILL SCHWIRZER
& LESLIE KAY

Roseville, CA

Printed in United States of America

All Rights Reserved
Published by Amazing Facts, Inc.
P. O. Box 1058
Roseville, CA 95678-8058
800-538-7275

Unless otherwise noted, Bible texts in the Introduction, Chapters One, Two, Three, Six, Eight, Nine, Twelve, Fourteen and Seventeen are from the New King James Version.

Unless otherwise noted, Bible texts in Chapters Four, Five, Seven, Ten, Eleven, Thirteen, Fifteen and Sixteen are from the New American Standard Bible.

Other books by Jennifer Jill Schwirzer:
Testimony of a Seeker
A Most Precious Message
I Want It All

Other books by Leslie Kay:
Scraps of Wisdom From Grasshopper Junction
Simple Gifts

Text Editing by Anthony Lester
Copy Editing by Arlene Clark
Cover Design by Haley Trimmer
Text Design and Layout by Greg Solie • AltamontGraphics.com

Typeset: 12/14 Minion

ISBN 10: 1-58019-177-0
ISBN 13: 978-1-58019-177-7

Library of Congress Cataloging-in-Publication Data

Schwirzer, Jennifer Jill, 1957-
  A deep but dazzling darkness : exploring God's "dark side" in the light of His love / Jennifer Jill Schwirzer, Leslie Kay.
    p. cm.
  Includes bibliographical references and index.
  ISBN 1-58019-177-0 (alk. paper)
  1. Judgment of God--History of doctrines. 2. God--Love--History of doctrines. I. Kay, Leslie (Leslie Eileen), 1957- II. Title.

BT180.J8S39 2004
231'.8--dc22

                              2004014876

08 09 10 11 • 5 4 3 2

Contents

Acknowledgments

With much appreciation for A. Leroy Moore, a gentleman and a scholar, who has challenged us to wrestle with truth in all its paradoxical beauty and to value what it means to be a vital part of the priesthood of believers.

Thanks to Anthony Lester for reading with a writer's heart and for his enthusiastic recommendation to the publishing team at Amazing Facts.

And with many grateful thanks to Nancy J. Vyhmeister and Herbert E. Douglass for their scholarly and editorial advice.

There is in God, some say,
A deep, but dazzling darkness; as men here
Say it is late and dusky, because they
See not all clear.

—Henry Vaughan,
Silex Scintillans, Part II [1655], The Night

Introduction

Blinded by the Light

*I*t is high noon. A child prances into her front yard. The lawn vibrates green, the sun dazzles, forcing a squinting smile upon her face. It promises to be a happy day. But a mischievous comrade joins her, breathing a secret that exposes the only danger for miles around: "I dare you to stare at the sun." The one enticed sways for a moment, contemplating the ramifications of both options before her. If she says no, her peer status might take an immediate nose-dive, possibly even resulting in being labeled a "chicken." If she says yes, the consequence would be twofold: a smarting conscience because of disobedience to mother's taboo, and the possible discovery that Mama was right after all.

"Staring at the sun hurts your eyes," she mumbles, embarrassed.

The ensuing barrage of taunts leads the child to reprioritize: She will risk disobedience and injury rather than suffer peer rejection. Fear of shame overrides fear of all other dangers. Her head slowly tips back, eyes clamped shut. As the darer adds pressure, the eyes part, squinting at first through a tangle of lashes. Taunts continue until finally the will to score socially triumphs over pain. Lids and lashes reach back like the opening petals of a flower. Finally, painfully, the raw energy of an orb that, although 93 million miles away, still contains 386 billion billion megawatts of energy strikes the eyes, bringing an instant chain reaction.

The unfiltered light enters the cornea-window, which begins to bend it toward the center of the eye. The iris isn't so compliant—it frantically contracts to let in as little of the devastating blaze as possible. Yet even at its most vigilant, the pupil is still open, a pinpoint entrance for the fire. Methodically, the sight of the sun is thrown to the back of the eye toward the retina, in which are the rods and cones—the "ink" of the eye. Responsible for color sensation, the cones ignore the white-hot sun, while the black-and-white sensing rods declare a red alert.

Now the phenomenon of light-induced blindness begins. Visual purple, the pigment in the eye's paintbrush, is bleached out by the luminous overload, rendering the rods incapable of image discernment. Fortunately, pain overcomes all other motives and the child looks away from what would have eventually brought her permanent damage. Because her visual purple cannot discern light or trace images, the world that only moments ago bloomed with brilliant color is now dark. She stumbles, groping for her friend's hand. She is left with a souvenir of her affair with folly: Where the bright orb of the sun burned into her retina, she sees nothing but a black ball projected on the backs of her lids.

Light brings sight, but light brings blindness. Is the light to blame? Has the sun become dark because our eyes have gone dark? No. It's still light. The hindrance to our ability to perceive the sun is not due to the sun itself, but to the inadequacies of the perceiving organ. When we try to see brilliant light, our eyes go dark, not with the darkness of the light itself, but with a darkness imposed by our frail sight mechanism.

"God is light" (1 John 1:5). His very being is uninterrupted luminescence. Yet we shrink from what we perceive to be His frighteningly "dark side" of justice and judgment, of wrath and condemnation. Could it also be that the fault is not in God, but in our fragile organs of spiritual perception? Could it be that as we strive to comprehend God's sterner, hard-to-understand attributes, we find ourselves groping in the darkness because our fallen perceptions have been overwhelmed and blinded by the light of His love?

Chapter One

In Him Is No Darkness

LESLIE'S STORY

*A*rchbishop Timothy Manning sat in state as he surveyed the current crop of confirmation recipients. Fresh-faced and white-robed, the class of 30 or so preteens nearly radiated impending sainthood. Behind them sat the doting parents and godparents, friends and extended family that had come to celebrate the occasion. Cameras ready, each focused on a single, all-important objective—getting a good shot of their respective little angel's moment of glory. And as the little angels nervously awaited that moment of glory, their thoughts were anxiously riveted on a single, dreaded event—the slap.

The famed slap had been the premier topic of conversation since the beginning of our confirmation class. "Did it hurt?" we wondered aloud. Did he really let you have it? Molly Maguire, who knew everything about anything, assured us with an air of authority, "My brother, Joe, said it doesn't feel like anything. The archbishop just says your confirmation name, sticks the oil on your forehead and barely even taps you on the cheeks. There's nothing to it."

I wasn't so sure. I'd never even been looked at by an archbishop, let alone slapped by one. (In public, no less.) And what about the oil? What were we supposed to *do* with the stuff? Molly had an answer. "You're *never* supposed to wash it off. It's holy oil. It's just supposed to stay there forever."

Simple enough, yet when my moment of truth came, I marched down the aisle with more than a little trepidation. Trembling, I handed Archbishop Manning the card bearing my confirmation name—Bernadette, my favorite from the pantheon of saints. Duly pronouncing me Bernadette, he dipped his thumb in olive oil, traced a sign of the cross on my forehead, then lightly slapped first one cheek, then the other. And that was it. Molly was right. It was rather perfunctory after all.

Truth be told, most of what constituted my early introduction to religion was much like that slap in the face— impersonal, illogical, and vaguely unfriendly. God was a nice guy, or so I was told. But I could never get close enough to Him to find out for sure. As far as I could tell, He was a distant, shadowy figure—approached through a multitude of saints, and appeased by a multitude of prayers. He was a vigilant scorekeeper who never missed an opportunity to put a black mark against your name, wiping it away only grudgingly when you'd rendered sufficient penance.

Even so, I wanted to believe that God was good at heart, and I loved Him to the best of my ability. I said my prayers dutifully and willingly. I sincerely wanted to know Him, but because we seldom cracked a Bible, I was clueless as to what His own Book said about Him. And the answers that my well-meaning catechism teachers provided just didn't add up, even based on logic. Why would God say, "It's not good for the man to be alone," then make Jesus live out His life a lonely celibate, deprived of the warmth and companionship of family? Why did Christ bother to die on the cross if people could atone for their own sins in a horrible place called purgatory? If God really wanted me to live with Him forever in heaven, why did He make it so hard for me to get there?

If God was good, why did He act so badly?

Disappointment blossomed into full-blown disillusionment soon after my confirmation. I left my church and rebelled for a time, then felt my lack of spiritual orientation and joined what I thought was a more user-friendly church. Warm and accepting, with a charismatic worship service that boasted lots of high-energy music and congregational participation, my new church was very different from the austere, ritualistic one of my childhood. However, along with the fellowship and vitality came an emphasis on eternal damnation that made the perils of purgatory sound tame. Our pastor wasn't shy when it came to preaching about it.

"Don't let anybody tell you that hell isn't a real place!" she'd thunder, with a vehemence that made her beehive hairdo tremble. "The Bible says that God will *punish* the immoral and the unbelieving with eternal hellfire while the redeemed look down approvingly from the walls of the New Jerusalem!"

The Bible sure *seemed* to say that; I didn't understand it well enough to conclude otherwise. But the more I thought about it, the more I realized I just couldn't love a God who roasted people alive for an unrelenting eternity. After months of painful deliberation, I decided that if that was what God was like, I wanted no part of Him. If hell was a real place, I resigned myself to going there. And along with my Bible, I tossed Christianity with its harsh, vindictive God into the dumpster and didn't look back.

My story of disillusionment and departure is not unique. It can be told many times over, by many different people, with as many variations as there are life experiences. And because keeping a story to herself has never been one of Jennifer's strengths, I'll let her have *her* say now.

Jennifer's Turn

Unlike Leslie's story, my early introduction to religion was pleasant enough. I remember it fondly as I look at a snapshot of me in my childhood choir. All 25 or so kids are displayed on the central staircase of the Aurora Inn, where our church had its Christmas concert that year. My face is glowing with hope and innocence; my hair lies freshly washed against my bright-red choir robe. In my hands is a glowing candle. In my eyes is a kind of holy rapture, as if singing the sweet strains of the hymns of the first advent had temporarily transformed me into an angel. As I look at myself through this Kodak time tunnel, I recall feeling transported to heaven itself.

I remember wanting to be holy and good as I sat dutifully in church beside the widow Mrs. Perkins, letting her call me her "pew pal" even though my brothers snickered. I remember coffee hour, where I could eat all kinds of rich, sweet donuts even though it wasn't breakfast time, and listen to the cacophony of the church women as their red-lipsticked lips vibrated with gossip. I remember winning the roll-a-potato-with-your-nose contest at the church picnic. Everything about church and religion was either pleasant or comical.

Then one day, my Sunday school teacher read the Ten Commandments, and religion suddenly became very dark. It wasn't the commandments that got to me; it was the motivation God enjoined for obedience to them. Right there in the heart of the second commandment it sat like a weed among the posies of my inner portrait of God: "For I the Lord Thy God am a *jealous* God."

"Jealous?" I thought, "How can God be *jealous*?" The thought struck my young mind as a contradiction in terms, like "colorless rainbow" or "dark sunbeam." God was everything soft, warm, and congenial. He epitomized what was right, pure, and innocent. Yet here He was laying claim to an emotion so dark that I was forbidden to harbor it. While jealousy lived only in my heart's inner recesses, repressed and regarded with guilt and shame, God was displaying His own jealousy as if it were something of which to be proud.

Because I attended a liberal, non-fundamentalist church, I had little exposure to the Bible, especially to those portions that smacked of "fire and brimstone." This first exposure, however, cued me in to liberal Christendom's skeleton in the closet—that, according to the Bible, God had what appeared to be a "dark side." I was at once repulsed and intrigued by it, yet didn't have a clue about how to reconcile it with the warm, fuzzy picture I'd been taught. It haunted me more than I realized.

My parents practiced a bedtime prayer ritual with us kids. Mom or Dad would enter our rooms, kneel by our beds and listen as we prayed a rote prayer with such speed that it was unintelligible to anyone who hadn't also memorized it. It wasn't exactly heartfelt communication with the Lord, but it served as a reassuring send-off to sleep. Yet after my introduction to God's "dark side," I couldn't melt into unconsciousness as usual. Instead, I would curl into a ball and work my way toward the hopeless request, "God, bless my grades at school and my art projects, and help me make money so I can buy Christmas presents … and please, God, tell me you are *not jealous!*"

As time went by, my God-concept problems were compounded by a developing personality conflict with my father. As far as kids are concerned, God and parents are rolled into one subconscious reality. Children aren't able to psychologically differentiate God from the authority figures in their lives, especially their fathers. The dynamic

I was developing with God was already etched out by my relationship with Dad, who also had a "dark side" I didn't understand.

Dad was an honest, hardworking, decent man with a million friends, a beautiful home, a stable marriage and a philosophy of parenting that was firmly rooted in "spare the rod, spoil the child." When I was a little girl, Dad's voice of reproof sent me flying to him, compulsively wrapping my arms around the highest point I could reach, which was right about at his knees. Fortunately, this was the mercy seat of his anatomy, and he didn't have the heart to punish a penitent child. This worked well until I reached adolescence, when I lost the inclination to humble myself in order to assuage his wrath. The result was repeated confrontation between two very headstrong personalities. I remember the verbal mortar fire, with our voices competing for supremacy until Dad finally overwhelmed me with sheer force of personality, size and volume.

I've since come to understand the impetus behind Dad's rage a little better. He was a mixed bag of fatherly concern and male ego. His hackles raised at things that would hurt his daughter, but his daughter herself often hurt his pride and rejected his authority. In my immaturity, I was blind to his better motives and saw his rage as nothing more than an offended ego. In my mind he said, "She's denying me and defying me. I'll terrify her into submission."

Only supernatural power can enable us to isolate the truth about God from the psychological impressions left by our usually-good-but-imperfect parents. At this stage of my life, I wasn't informed by the Holy Spirit, except for those serendipitous moments when a nameless Savior spoke, moments that were subsequently lost to other influences. Spurred for the most part by the whims of compulsive sinful nature, I did what we all do: I subconsciously assumed that the same megalomaniac ego that leads human beings to exploit rage for their own purposes was present in the

God of Christianity—the God who dared to be jealous, restrictive, punitive and even wrathful. When I left home for good at 18, I also left behind the religion that countenanced such negativity.

BEATING A PATH

So there you have it. Though our stories differ in the details, and were experienced half a continent apart, decades before we met each other, we came to identical conclusions. As far as we could tell, Christianity was an inconsistent, illogical religion, and its God was a demanding, unpredictable control freak who required much of His subjects and gave little in return. Integrity seemed to require that we reject them both.

Yet jettisoning our Christianity left us with a spiritual vacuum that insisted on being filled with some sort of spiritual orientation; New Age alternatives seemed to provide the answer. So we exchanged our negative, arbitrary God for a detached but benevolent energy force that didn't keep score or throw temper tantrums. Only the names were changed as we experimented with first one, then another version of this god. Buddha, Krishna, the Goddess—all these icons embodied the same dispassionate force that regarded us with supreme disinterest, even as we passionately beat a path to their respective doors. As time went by, the irony of our predicament sank in: The same impassiveness that made these gods incapable of negativity also made them incapable of giving and receiving love. All of which ultimately brought us full circle back to Christianity, to the only God who seemed passionate enough to love us the way we needed to be loved.

We've found, since coming back, that we're not the only ones who have struggled to understand and accept God's "darker" attributes. We've watched many brothers and sisters wrestle with divine wrath, jealousy and condemnation, just as we have. We've watched many reject the God of Christianity as we did, because they'd received a distorted picture of these sterner attributes, a picture that had been severed from the anchor of His unselfish love. And we've seen an equally disturbing phenomenon, a compensatory pendulum swing in the opposite direction—the "positivization" of God. We've seen the importation into the church of New Age concepts that artificially sweeten and soften God's sterner attributes, depriving Him, who is love, of the full range of passionate action and emotion that expression of His love requires.

We'd like to share with these struggling brothers and sisters, and with other honest-hearted seekers, something of what we've learned through our own wrestlings—that there is a biblical alternative to the human extremes of rejecting or positivizing the "dark side" of God's love. To discover it, we must determine not to allow people, institutions, or our own biases to define the parameters of that love. We must subjugate human reason and wisdom to the inspired Word, which alone can clarify that which is obscure to us.

The Bible says, "God is light, and in him is no darkness at all" (1 John 1:5 KJV). Could it be that what our mortal "eyes" interpret as God's darkness is really part of the brilliant spectrum of His love? Could it be that we just don't naturally possess the spiritual faculties to take in something so brilliant? If so, then the problem is not in the Word of God, the wrath of God or the jealousy of God, but in us. We need supernaturally strengthened spiritual perceptions, that we may see the love in each and every act of God, whether it is Jesus receiving a flower from a child or Jehovah commanding every child of Jericho to be "utterly destroyed" (Joshua 6:21).

When we allow the Holy Spirit to strengthen our spiritual perceptions, we'll see that the Bible is not a book about God, per se; it's a book about God's dealings with sin and sinners. Because of this, it doesn't focus on His perfect life in heaven before sin, but on His trials and tribulations after sin. In the Bible, we see God, not so much in His finest garments, though there are those snapshots here and there. We see Him in His work clothes, up to His elbows in the muck and mire of a mess called sin. As He condescends to patiently involve Himself in that which He could obliterate, He lets sin, and His reaction to it, muddy up His public image.

Why does He take such a risk? Is it because He wants things His way, and He'll do whatever it takes to get it? Not at all. God risks being misunderstood and vilified for His "negativity" because His selfless love mandates that He take action against that which would cause our ruin. Jealousy, wrath, condemnation, judgment, punishment, all of these seemingly harsh attributes and actions find their wellspring in God's holy love. Because sin is a destroyer, God's protective, discriminating "dark side" is goaded into action by it. Yet although our sin-created state of emergency might goad God into stepping outside of His comfort zone, it can never force Him to step outside of His character. Essentially, internally, He who is love remains the same "yesterday, today, and forever" (Hebrews 13:8). So the eternal Father plays the part of the divine disciplinarian, as He takes responsibility for a crisis not of His own making.

It's a dilemma to which every parent can relate. No loving parent enjoys playing the heavy. We've all experienced the sense of defeat that gnaws at our fragile parental self-esteem at the end of a hard day of hand-to-hand combat. We've sent our kids to bed in utter frustration, only to find ourselves drawn to their bedside, watching them drift off to sleep. As the tension dissolves from their faces and their features grow mellow with innocence, our hearts melt with tenderness and affection. *How could I have been angry with you?* we wonder. *Tomorrow will be a better day; you'll be good and I won't have to punish*, we vow, as we plant a lingering kiss on their cheek. Yet the next day, as the little rascals repeatedly yank us out of doting-parent mode into punitive-parent mode, we remember what we managed to forget as we watched them slumber. We wish it could be otherwise.

So does God. He wishes we would allow Him to be our friend instead of forcing Him to be our reprover. He'd rather give out kisses than spankings, and hugs more than hard words. "He does not willingly afflict or grieve the sons of men" (Lamentations 3:33 RSV). However, the love that carves deep rivers of affection for all His erring children also harbors deep antipathy toward that which would draw them even farther away from Him. So He perseveres with us.

As we embark upon this journey through God's "dark side," tracing the origin and development of sin and His sometimes-puzzling reactions to it, may His Spirit anoint our eyes that we may discern the love from which they spring. May we who are accustomed to dwelling in darkness be strengthened to bear the brightness of the full spectrum of that love, that we will not be blinded, but drawn "out of [our] darkness into His marvelous light" (1 Peter 2:9 RSV).

Chapter Two

Rebel Without a Cause

rench poet and playwright Jean Cocteau wrote, "I like imaginary stories better than history, whose truths eventually lose their shape. The lies in stories eventually become a kind of truth or, at least, a mysterious, new, and delightful form of history."[1] These words especially described one of Cocteau's favorite imaginary stories, *Beauty and the Beast*, the classic fairy tale of redeeming love that transformed a hideous beast into a noble prince.

Yet if "the lies in stories eventually become a kind of truth," it is because they trace their twisted roots to some facet of truth, which is itself often stranger than the fiction it spawns. The story of redeeming love that has power to transform virtual beasts into noble princes and princesses is the meta-narrative of the Bible. And it's preceded and necessitated by its antagonistic inverse—the story of a majestic angel who, surrounded by the undimmed brilliance of that love, stubbornly transformed himself from a noble prince into a virtual beast.

No logical reason can be given for this perverse transformation. The "mystery of iniquity" defies rational explanation; to excuse it is to justify it (2 Thessalonians 2:7

KJV). It was and still is an anomaly in God's otherwise perfect universe, a rogue outburst of "lawlessness" against the law of self-giving love that God instilled within His creation. (1 John 3:4). Yet though we can never know the *why* of sin, we can at least learn something of the *how* of it, as we trace this once majestic angel's monumental fall from grace.

How the Mighty Have Fallen

According to God, "Lucifer, son of the morning," was "the seal of perfection, Full of wisdom and perfect in beauty" (Isaiah 14:12; Ezekiel 28:12). Animated by the same spirit of selfless love that prompted his Creator, he was "perfect in [his] ways from the day [he] was created" (Ezekiel 28:15). Nothing that a holy heart could desire was withheld from him, as he "walked back and forth in the midst of fiery stones"—that is, strode freely about in the fiery presence of God Himself (Ezekiel 28:14; see Revelation 4:2, 3; Exodus 24:9, 10).

First among the angels, *helel ben-shachar,* Hebrew for "Shining one, son of the morning," was second in splendor only to Christ, the self-existent "Bright and Morning Star" (Revelation 22:16). In fact, the similarities between the two are striking—Lucifer, whose name means "light bearer," was the closest created approximation to Christ, called in 2 Peter 1:19 the *phosphoros,* "morning star;" literally, the "light bearer." A fit companion for divinity, he was all that divinity could devise—brilliant, loving, free, and willingly attuned to the character of his Creator and Sustainer.

So Lucifer's heart beat in unison with the great heart of God, until the unthinkable happened. Gradually, almost imperceptibly, his "heart became proud on account of [his] beauty, and [he] corrupted [his] wisdom because of [his] splendor" (Ezekiel 28:17 NIV). Inexplicably, inexcusably, "*iniquity* was found in" him—an internal bending or twisting away from the actuating principle of selflessness to its antagonistic principle of self-exaltation (Ezekiel 28:15).[2] "Malignant narcissism," characterized by a "willful failure of submission,"[3] began to subtly assert itself. No longer calibrated to the universal pulse of "not my will, but thine, be done" (Luke 22:42 KJV), Lucifer's overmastering impulse became *"I will"*—

> "*I will* ascend into heaven,
> *I will* exalt my throne above the [angels] of God;
> *I will* also sit on the mount of the congregation On the farthest sides of the north;
> *I will* ascend above the heights of the clouds,
> *I will* be like the Most High" (Isaiah 14:13–15 emphasis supplied).

Though this satanic declaration of independence was at first whispered only in the private recesses of Lucifer's heart (v. 13), God was aware of it. More specifically, Christ was painfully aware of it, as Lucifer's rivalry was most pointedly directed toward Him. No longer content to be the "*son* of the morning," he aspired to the power and position of the "bright and morning star" Himself. It was an insane ambition, to be sure—to think that *he*, a dependent, created being, could supplant his Creator and Sustainer. To think that *he* could "sit on the mount of the congregation"—occupy the very throne of God—and orchestrate the workings of a thousand spinning galaxies. Yet so blinded had he become by his pathological pride, so "corrupted" had become his wisdom, that he was bereft of sense. And so enslaved had he become to his insatiable ambition to be worshiped that he resolved to do whatever it took to amass an army of converts to his "cause."

You Say You Want a Revolution

So began the revolution. Adolf Hitler, who knew a thing or two about revolutions, asserted in his manifesto *Mein Kampf,*

"The great masses of people ... will more easily fall victims to a big lie than to a small one."[4] Lucifer, whom Jesus called the "father" of lies, understood how to make a big lie palatable (John 8:44). He understood that the most successful revolutions are not established overtly, but covertly—subtly, seductively, almost imperceptibly. So he set about to seduce into cultic conformity a core group of fanatic followers.

Skillfully, Lucifer began to weave his own spiritual and mental illness into the social fabric of heaven. Stealthily, he introduced his "big lie" about the Creator. God was not who He appeared to be, he asserted; He was not what He claimed—"merciful and gracious, long-suffering, and abounding in goodness and truth" (Exodus 34:6). A sinister purpose lurked behind His benevolent countenance; a tyrannical agenda lay back of His apparently gracious dealings. According to Lucifer, God was intrinsically, incurably flawed, and He could not be trusted.

This monstrous lie, Lucifer wrapped in velvet. Cloaking himself in the soft, subtle folds of sanctimony, he feigned loyalty to God even while he undermined it. It pained him to say such things about his Creator, he insisted. He wouldn't even say them if he didn't have his fellow angels' best interest in mind. His passive-aggressive sales pitch, which has been echoed by countless demagogues and gurus from time immemorial, may well have sounded something like this:

"It's not that I'm trying to discredit God. He's been good to us—so far. As long as we've bowed to His authority. But why should such wise and holy beings bow to an authority outside of ourselves? Why should unnecessary, externally imposed laws curtail our rightful liberty? There is a more exalted state beyond that which we've been permitted to experience. If you adopt me as your spiritual leader, I will humbly do my best to facilitate your entrance into that experience."

Assiduously, he drew his listeners out, urging them to lay claim to a discontent they had never before known, instilling within them a yearning for an indefinable something they had never before needed. He aroused self-will where none had previously exerted itself. Masterfully exploiting their affection for him, he persuaded them to transfer their allegiance from God to himself, without their even recognizing how it happened. And even as he wreaked all this heavenly havoc, he charged all the trouble on God.

That he won a third of the angels to his cause, and left the remainder bewildered by his sophistry, is testimony to the success of his strategy and persistence (see Revelation 12:4). The Bible portrays him as a kind of traveling salesman, doggedly pounding the streets of heaven, peddling his poisonous wares: "By the abundance of your trading You became filled with violence within, And you sinned" (Ezekiel 28:16). The more he vented his discontent, the more converts he won, the more he became "filled with violence"— filled with the turmoil and intoxication of self-love.

Yet God bore long with Lucifer. The One whose "mercy is everlasting," whose "compassions fail not," was willing to forgive and reinstate His fallen angel (Psalm 100:5; Lamentations 3:22). Patiently He reasoned, pointing out Lucifer's fatal flaw of pride and where it would lead—to eternal destruction to himself and to all who would fall under his spell. But Lucifer had lost his appetite for truth. As he gave himself over to this mysterious evil, the pain of self-revelation became intolerable. As M. Scott Peck has observed, "What distinguishes the evil" is that there is "one particular kind of pain they cannot tolerate: the pain of their own conscience, the pain of the realization of their own sinfulness and imperfection."[5] Rejecting the redemption implicit in that pain, Lucifer, the heavenly "light bearer," became Satan, the implacable "adversary" of God and all things created.

The transformation was complete. By his own perverse, persistent choice, the once noble prince had become a raging beast. The seed of disaffection he had nourished in his heart had matured into the vile plant of full-blown rebellion. So

Satan unfit himself for a holy heaven, and as there was no more place for him, he was "cast ... as a profane thing Out of the mountain of God" (Ezekiel 28:16).

The book of Revelation describes this cosmic confrontation between opposing spirits and their ideologies in these words:

> "War broke out in heaven: Michael[6] [Christ] and his angels fought with the dragon; and the dragon and his angels fought, but they did not prevail, nor was a place found for them in heaven any longer. So the great dragon was cast out, that serpent of old, called the Devil and Satan, who deceives the whole world; he was cast to the earth, and his angels were cast out with him" (Revelation 12:7–9).

THREE LITTLE WORDS

It's at this juncture that we probably feel like sitting back, heaving a collective sigh of disgust and muttering, "Thanks a lot, God. Of all the places you could have thrown him, why did you have to throw him *here?*" And we could go further. If God knew this pathological "father of lies" was also "a murderer from the beginning," why did He let him live at all (John 8:44 NIV)? Why didn't He just vaporize the big liar and his imps with one blinding masterstroke?

These are good questions. And the short answer to all of them is contained in three potent little words: *freedom of choice.*

"God is love" is the biblical equation, and one of the most defining characteristics of love is its unfailing respect for the freedom of choice of its beloved (1 John 4:8). Never does it, nor can it, force the will. God doesn't want a universe of mindless automatons; He wants friends. So when He created beings with the capacity for friendship, He had to also equip them with the capacity (though not the predisposition) for enmity. This means that, just as holy but free angels couldn't be forced to love God, holy and free humanity could not be forced to hate Him. We didn't have to sympathize with the devil.

The way in which this love-mandated freedom of choice plays into God's tolerance of evil can be illustrated in the rise and fall of Adolf Hitler, eminently successful purveyor of the "big lie."

Post-World War I Germany provided fertile ground for a totalitarian revolution. Already humiliated by its defeat, dispirited by its territorial losses and strapped by its reparation payments, by 1923 Germany was stressed almost beyond measure by runaway inflation. Capitalizing on the instability and popular discontent, Hitler unsuccessfully attempted a military coup, for which he was arrested and jailed. He learned from this experience that democracy is best destroyed, not by outside force, but by building up popular support from within the system.

Styling himself a savior of his downtrodden people, Hitler played upon their wounded national pride and discontent, and gradually rose to power within the democratic government. Assisted by the worldwide depression and the collapse of the German economy, which his party helped to manipulate, he established himself as Germany's absolute totalitarian dictator by 1933. To his people, he was a messiah. To the democratic world, he was a worrisome enigma to be puzzled over and, for a time, appeased. Another global war and more than 60 million deaths later,[7] the world reeled as it recognized in him a virtual personification of evil. It can be argued that in his writings and even his earliest political behavior, Hitler gave the world ample cause to fear him.[8] On the other hand, what decent person could have truly anticipated the unbelievable monster he would turn out to be?

Just so, though the angels were forewarned about where Lucifer was tending, and humanity was forewarned about what he had so far become, none could fully discern where his lies would ultimately take him. None could fathom the potential for evil that coiled in the heart of this mad visionary who, like Hitler, was "simultaneously obsessed with fantastic visions and blinded to reality by those very visions."[9] None but God. He who discerns "the end from the beginning, And from ancient times things that are not yet done" foresaw the heartache and destruction this fallen angel would wreak on His universe (Isaiah 46:10). Yet if He had peremptorily terminated Satan's bid for power, even out of love for His vulnerable creation, He would have destroyed his presence at the expense of immortalizing his influence.

Nothing has greater power than an idea. Once planted in the fertile soil of the mind, ideas are as seed that, in time, bring forth a certain harvest. Satan had broadcast the seeds of doubt and confusion: *Was God really arbitrary and tyrannical? Was He withholding from His creatures a freer, more exalted state of being? Was Satan really a misunderstood messiah who just needed a break?* Such serious assertions take time to consider; such potent ideas insist on being either affirmed or invalidated. If God had derailed this process of reasoning from cause to effect and prevented these ideas from coming to fruition, He would have succeeded in establishing the very instability He sought to correct.

Worse yet, if He had summarily executed this rebel without a cause, He would have done more than instill a legacy of doubt. He would have introduced another strange, new element into His universe—the motivation of fear. He would have given every created intelligence the unmistakable message—*If you step out of line, the same will happen to you.* And just as love cannot use force to win affectionate cooperation, it cannot and will not use fear to do the same. So God enmeshed Himself in the heart-sickening dilemma initiated by sin.

As it took a ruinous war finally fought on its own soil to inoculate Germany against totalitarianism, so it would take a ruinous war against sin to inoculate men and angels against its horrors. The seeds of destruction must be allowed to sprout and bear the rotting fruit of death. The "mystery of iniquity" must be freely and intelligently rejected. After the principle of sin had been discredited, then its tragic residue could be destroyed.

But first, the revolution would ignite this beautiful blue planet.

Endnotes

1. Jean Cocteau, from the Afterword to Marie Leprince de Beaumont's *Beauty and the Beast* (Simon & Schuster Books for Young Readers, 1990), p. 35.

2. "Sin," wrote Dr. Karl Menninger in his book *Whatever Became of Sin?*, "has a willful, defiant or disloyal quality, *someone* is defied or offended or hurt. The willful disregard or sacrifice of the welfare of others for the welfare or satisfaction of the self is an essential quality of the concept of *sin*. St. Augustine described it as a turning 'away from the universal whole to the individual part. ... There is nothing greater [i.e., more important, more desirable, more worthy] than the whole. Hence when he desires [seeks, devotes himself to] something greater, he grows smaller.' And sin is thus, at heart, a refusal of the love of others." Karl Menninger, *Whatever Became of Sin?* (New York: Hawthorn Books, 1973), p. 19; emphases in original. (St. Augustine quoted from *De Trinitate*, XII, 14, as quoted in the Dutch Roman Catholic catechism.)

3. M. Scott Peck, *People of the Lie* (New York: Simon & Schuster, 1983), p. 79.

4. Adolf Hitler, *Mein Kampf*, as quoted in *Bartlett's Familiar Quotations*, Sixteenth Edition.

5. Peck, p. 77.

6. Hebrew, *Mika'el*, "Who [is] like God?" Although Michael is not explicitly identified as Christ in any one passage of Scripture, a comparison of various passages makes this identification clear. Jude 9 identifies Michael as "the archangel;" 1 Thessalonians 4:16 associates the resurrection of the saints at the coming of Jesus with "the voice of the archangel;" and finally, in John 5:28, Jesus declares that it is His voice that will call the dead from their graves. Thus, Christ is Michael the archangel, or "chief of the angels."

7. This figure encompasses the total worldwide loss of life in all theaters of combat, and includes the victims of the Holocaust.

8. In his Introduction to the Houghton Mifflin American translation of *Mein Kampf*, Konrad Heiden wrote, "For years *Mein Kampf* stood as proof of the blindness and complacency of the world. For in its pages Hitler announced—long before he came to power—a program of blood and terror in a self-revelation of such overwhelming frankness that few among its readers had the courage to believe it. Once again it was demonstrated that there was no more effective method of concealment than the broadest publicity." (Boston: Houghton Mifflin, 1943), p. xv.

9. From "Hitler, Adolf," Microsoft Encarta Online Encyclopedia 2001 http://encarta.msn.com copyright 1997–2000 Microsoft Corporation, All Rights Reserved.

Chapter Three

Paradise Lost

Of Man's first disobedience, and the fruit
Of that forbidden tree whose mortal taste
Brought death into the world, and all our woe,
With loss of Eden.
—John Milton, *Paradise Lost*, book 1, line 1[1]

The human race hasn't always wandered restlessly from place to place, searching for a familiar piece of ground. We haven't always been vagabonds in the earth. There was a time when we had a home. A time when we knew where we belonged, and to whom we belonged.

"And the Lord God planted a garden eastward in Eden; and there he put the man whom he had formed" (Genesis 2:8 KJV). This man, Adam, whose name means "of the ground," was placed in the midst of that familiar ground from which he'd been formed, "to till it and keep it" (Genesis 2:15 RSV). So Adam understood life's few fundamentals: He knew what he was made of and Who had made him; he knew where his home was, and what he was to do in it. And he knew one thing more—that the love with which God had infused him at his creation must be shared with another, comparable to himself.

So God set about to make him a soul mate, and in so doing completed the reflection of His image in humanity. Reaching deep into Adam's very structure, He gently withdrew a rib from which He fashioned Eve, who would become "the mother of all living" (Genesis 3:20). And as He had done with Adam, He "breathed into [her] nostrils the breath of life; and [she] became a living being"[2] (Genesis 2:7). When Adam saw her, he exclaimed in an ecstasy of gratitude and admiration, "This is now bone of my bones And flesh of my flesh; She shall be called Woman, Because she was taken out of Man" (Genesis 2:23). God joined them together in marriage, and they became one flesh. "And they were both naked, the man and his wife, and were not ashamed" (Genesis 2:25).

So they passed their days, working and loving, and worshiping God in every thought and act. Absolutely in harmony with His character of self-controlled, self-giving love, they drank in His presence like life itself, for so it was to them. God came first in their love and in their thought, "and that without painful effort. In perfect cyclic movement, being, power and joy descended from God to man in the form of gift and returned from man to God in the form of obedient love and ecstatic adoration."[3] Created in His self-forgetful image, they possessed no natural resistance to surrendering themselves to Him. Their "*data*, so to speak, were a psycho-physical organism wholly subject to the will and a will wholly disposed, though not compelled, to turn to God. The self-surrender which [they] practiced before the Fall meant no struggle but only the delicious overcoming of an infinitesimal self-adherence which delighted to be overcome—of which we see a dim analogy in the rapturous mutual self-surrenders of lovers even now."[4]

Yet implicit in this capacity for rapturous self-surrender is the potential, though not the predisposition, for rampant self-indulgence, because as soon as there is a self, there is the potential for self-idolatry. There is the very real possibility that all the gifts, the powers and passions with which God has so generously endowed the self, will be exploited at His expense. Free moral agents are just that—free to choose to surrender themselves to, or sever themselves from, the care and authority of the One who has made them in His image. According to C. S. Lewis, "This is, if you like, the 'weak spot' in the very nature of creation, the risk which God apparently thinks worth taking."[5]

Having already been spurned by a third of the heavenly host, it was a risk with which God had become painfully familiar. Yet He thought it worth taking again, for love mandated that it be taken. Compelled by love, God first created angels, then a human family with whom to share Himself. Constrained by that same love, He equipped each one with the capacity to reject Him. Even as He tenderly fashioned us in His image, sculpted our lips and brushed on our eyelashes, His all-seeing eye traced our turbulent future; traced His own immeasurable heartache. Yet He could not find it within Himself to eradicate the "weak spot" and eliminate the risk. We would be made, and we would be free to serve or rebel against our Maker.

A TALE OF TWO TREES

Satan well knew that God's character would not permit Him to create beings compelled to serve Him cravenly or mindlessly. He well knew "the 'weak spot' in the very nature of creation." Having already exploited it in a third of his fellow angels, he now prepared to take advantage of it in the newest members of God's family. As he watched their innocent bliss, he saw an earthly portrayal of the heavenly paradise he had forfeited, and he was inflamed with envy. Nearly choking at the thought, he envisioned an entire race of such beings effortlessly reflecting the image of the One he so desperately hated, filling the earth with righteousness and light. *This will never do*, he seethed. *I must corrupt them at the start, in their infancy, and claim their dominion as my own.* To this end he bent his prodigious powers of persuasion and deception.

For all that the Bible appears to say about it, one might think God had left Adam and Eve at his mercy, unwarned and unprepared. But if we read between the lines, we'll see that God didn't abandon them as sheep to the slaughter. "Walking in the garden in the cool of the day," He came to visit with them, to explain the wonders of creation, and to instruct them about the nature of His government and Satan's rebellion against it (Genesis 3:8). The One whose policy throughout history has been to do "nothing, Unless He reveals His secret to His servants the prophets" would not have left His first children uninformed about their mortal enemy (Amos 3:7). And then, tucked away in His instruction about the garden— that they "till it and *keep* it"—is an implicit warning that is lost sight of in our English translation. The Hebrew verb *shamar*, translated "keep," means to guard, to watch, preserve, hold fast. Adam and Eve were made to understand that they had been given something precious, that it needed to be cherished and protected from a wily predator who would put forth every effort to defraud them of it.

Thankfully, this predator would not be allowed to dog their steps, continually tempting and harassing them; for also tucked away in God's instruction about the garden is the implied assurance that Satan's influence would be limited:

> "And out of the ground the Lord God made every tree grow that is pleasant to the sight and good for food. The tree of life was also in the midst of the garden, and the tree of the knowledge of good and evil. ... And the Lord God commanded the man, saying, 'Of every tree of the garden you may freely eat; but of the tree of the knowledge of good and evil you shall not eat, for in the day that you eat of it you shall surely die'" (Genesis 2:9, 16, 17).

Clearly, there was but one testing ground in the garden. Satan would be restricted to peddling his poisonous principles from the tree of the knowledge of good and evil. Should Adam and Eve become dissatisfied with all that God had graciously given them and entertain a fascination for its forbidden fruit, purposely gravitating toward it, they would place themselves on Satan's vantage ground. It was their only prohibition in an otherwise limitless landscape of sustenance and beauty. Yet why the need for this enigmatic tree, and its equally mysterious companion, the tree of life? Why complicate the beautiful simplicity of what was, humanly speaking, an otherwise perfect paradise?

These two trees illustrate two fundamental truths of human nature. First, human beings are not innately immortal. Every time Adam and Eve reached out their hands and were nourished by the tree of life, they exercised faith in God as the source of their immortality. They demonstrated that they understood that God "alone has immortality," in the inalienable sense, and that He alone could, moment by moment, sustain them in it (1 Timothy 6:16). Conversely, they also recognized that their continuance in immortality depended upon their *not* doing something—not eating of the tree of the knowledge of good and evil. God had said, "In the day that you eat of it, you shall surely die,"[6] not because the fruit was deadly—because everything He had made was life-giving and "very good"—but because such a demonstration of rebellious unbelief was tantamount to severing themselves from their life source.[7]

Second, and more to the point, the existence of these two trees indicates that human beings are not innately righteous. Righteousness, the state of being in harmony with God's universal law of unselfish, moral uprightness—of literally being morally "straight"—is ever and only derived from God.[8] This is the deeper truth of conditional immortality, the condition upon which immortality must be based. The Scriptures are clear that "the Spirit is life because of *righteousness*" (Romans 8:10 emphasis supplied). "Righteousness and justice are the foundation of [God's] throne," the source of His life-giving authority (Psalms 97:2). Without righteousness there can be no life, because righteousness is the fertile soil from which the plant of life springs.

Life is not a right; it's a privilege granted on condition of willing submission to the principles that sustain it. As long as Adam and Eve consented by faith to base the formation of their characters on God's life-promoting principles of righteousness, they could be entrusted with the gift of life. Should they choose against these principles, believing that they could somehow better themselves by reaching "beyond" righteousness to a knowledge bereft of it, they would disqualify themselves from receiving the priceless gift and experience death by default.

Toward this deadly end, Satan brought to bear his arsenal of mind control methods—the same methods, in principle, that he had so successfully used against his angelic companions. Fascinatingly, these same methods have in essence been employed by every cult, totalitarian regime and seductive culture throughout history.[9]

MIRACLE, MYSTERY AND AUTHORITY

Fyodor Dostoevsky describes these methods with chilling clarity in his novel, *The Brothers Karamazov*. In the chapter "The Grand Inquisitor," he paints a poetic parable in which Jesus appears during the Spanish Inquisition and is imprisoned as a heretic by the Grand Inquisitor. After informing the unresisting Jesus that He will be burned at the stake the following day, the Inquisitor gives the reason for His condemnation: "You see, then, You Yourself sowed the seeds of destruction for Your own kingdom, and no one else is to blame. And think now; was this the best that You could offer [humanity]? There are three forces, only three, on this earth that can overcome and capture once and for all the conscience of these feeble, undisciplined creatures, so as to give them happiness. These forces are *miracle, mystery and authority*. You rejected the first, the second, and the third of these forces and set up Your rejection as an example to men."[10]

These three forces, the Inquisitor asserts, Satan "offered" Christ in the wilderness temptation. But Christ, choosing to found His kingdom on the three life-giving principles of faith, freedom and love, refused any form of force or manipulation, utterly rejecting them. These three forces of death-dealing deceit Satan successfully exerted against Eve.

The miracle: Temptation has a supernatural element. Absently strolling through her exquisite garden home, Eve suddenly found herself confronting the forbidden tree. Perceiving herself to be alone and in no immediate danger, she lingered to consider its fragrant beauty, its desirability, its delicious mystery. All at once, she was not alone. Miraculously, a glittering serpent spoke. Not only that, he seemed to intuit her very thoughts as he echoed them back to her in musical, mesmerizing tones: "Has God indeed said, 'You shall not eat of every tree of the garden?'" (Genesis 3:1).

Here was a miracle, indeed! From the tree that should have sheltered her enemy, she is unexpectedly engaged by an enchanting creature who has apparently received from its fruit the power of speech. What a captivating introduction! How well Satan understood what history has repeatedly borne out—that "the suspension of 'natural and ordinary' routines, to produce an atmosphere of awe, is implicit in the ideology of every cult"[11]—and every cult-style seduction. Eve could have fled from the spot at once. Instead, she trusted her ability to handle what God had already told her was too big for her and stayed to parley with the devil.

The mystery: The enemy's design is to confuse the mind through unbelief. Undulating through the serpent's words, "Has God indeed said, 'You shall not eat of every tree of the garden?'" was a curious and confusing ambiguity. The Hebrew can be understood to mean either, "Has God really said, 'You shall not eat of *every* tree of the garden'?" or, "Has God really said, 'You shall not eat of *any* tree of the garden'?" The ambiguity was apparently intentional, calculated to confuse Eve by shrouding in mystery God's simple command, to focus her attention on what He was apparently withholding from her, and to entice a response.

Eve gamely replied, "We may eat the fruit of the trees of the garden; but of the fruit of the tree which is in the midst of the garden, God has said, 'You shall not eat it, nor shall you touch it, lest you die' " (Genesis 3:2, 3).

On the surface, her response appears to be confident enough. But closer scrutiny reveals her crumbling sense of clarity. God had unequivocally said, "Of the tree of the knowledge of good and evil you shall not eat, for in the day that you eat of it you shall *surely* die." Facilitated by the devil's mind-bending manipulations, God's definitive statement had become softened and blurred in Eve's mind to mean, "You shall not eat it ... *lest* you die"—which is comparable to saying, "*because you might* die," or, "*for fear that* you should die." Eve was beginning to free fall into the spiral of unbelief. As she doubted God's plain statements and entertained the unthinkable, her mind began to wobble away from the simple, love-inspired logic of obedience into the convoluted, destabilizing logic of disobedience. Satan instantly capitalized on her disorientation by unleashing the last phase of his plan—

The authority: Satan ultimately usurps God's sovereignty. Certain that his captive was fast in his snare, Satan authoritatively spewed out his big lie, "*You will not surely die.* For God knows that in the day you eat of it your eyes will be opened, and you will be like God, knowing good and evil" (Genesis 3:4, 5, emphasis supplied).

With these two brief sentences, Satan effectively reduced to rubble the divinely designed template for Eve's self-perception and worldview, replacing it with his own fundamentally flawed pattern. "God is a liar and a tyrant," he charged in effect, just as he had done in heaven. "You are innately immortal and don't need Him to sustain you. Your ultimate happiness will only be realized by rebelling against His restrictive principles of righteousness and severing all connection with Him. It's of no value to be good; life is all about *power*—the intoxicating power of knowledge and self-will. God knows that when you get that kind of power, you will become His equal."

Wrapped around his big lie of innate immortality, Satan had injected another subtle, mind-bending twist of ambiguity. Even as he asserted humanity's inherent right to life, he undermined the foundation on which that life is based. Disparaging righteousness, he replaced it with rebellion; disparaging God's sovereignty, he displaced it with his own spurious authority.

Eve bought it wholesale. Having transferred her confidence from her Creator to this created, self-appointed usurper, she had become putty in his hands. With the seductive elements of the "mystery of iniquity" now fully aroused and operative within her, she regarded the forbidden tree through vastly different eyes. Perceiving now that "the tree was good for food, that it was pleasant to the eyes, and a tree desirable to make one wise, she took of its fruit and ate" (Genesis 3:6).

EYES WIDE OPEN

Surely no convert is more enthusiastic than a new convert. Filling her arms with the forbidden fruit, Eve flew to Adam's side and breathlessly bubbled over with her newfound "faith." We can only imagine what transpired between them, as the Scriptures are silent. This much we're told: "Adam was not deceived, but the woman was deceived and became a transgressor" (1 Timothy 2:14 RSV). Eve had been deceived, however willingly, but Adam was not. As he considered her questionable "conversion" and regarded her hyper-stimulated "exalted state," he saw clearly what had happened. Eve had sinned, and he had lost her forever. His soul mate, his second self, she who had been made bone of his bones and flesh of his flesh, had eternally severed herself from God—and from him. She would die, and he would never share her delightful company again. Unable to fathom how he would live without her, unwilling to submit his heartache to God, Adam determined to die with her. Desperately he took the fruit and ate.

"Then the eyes of both of them were opened, and they knew that they were naked" (Genesis 3:7). Their eyes were opened, but they did not become as God, whose eyes view evil through the clarifying lens of uncorrupted righteousness. Their eyes were opened to evil by way of immersing themselves in it, giving themselves up to its perverting influence, in the process becoming its slaves. They now saw evil up close and personal, through the distorted, myopic lens of corrupted righteousness, and they didn't like the way it had changed their world. They saw with terrifying vividness their nakedness of soul, their innocence lost, their forfeited birthright. They saw their precious friendship become a source of confusion and blame as their pure, selfless love died, sacrificed on the altar of self-centeredness.

Endnotes

1. John Milton, *Paradise Lost and Other Poems* (Roslyn, NY: Walter J. Black, Inc., 1971), p. 91.

2. The Hebrew phrase *chai nephesh,* rendered "living being" in the NKJV, is synonymous with the phrase "living soul" in the KJV, indicating that a "soul" was not something placed *within* Adam and Eve, but was something they *became* as God animated them with His life.

3. C.S. Lewis, *The Problem of Pain* (New York: HarperCollins Publishers, Inc., 1996), p. 74.

4. *Ibid.,* p. 76.

5. *Ibid.*

6. Literally, in the Hebrew, "In the day that you eat of it, *to die you shall die*," meaning that if Adam and Eve should disobey, sentence would immediately be pronounced upon them, ultimately resulting in their death. Their status would be changed from that of conditional immortality to unconditional mortality.

7. For a fascinating, biblical, and exhaustively researched study on the subject, see Edward William Fudge, *The Fire That Consumes: The Biblical Case for Conditional Immortality* (Carlisle, UK: The Paternoster Press, 1994).

8. This is the moral "straightness" from which Lucifer diverged when he gave himself over to *iniquity*—the internal bending or twisting away from God's actuating principle of unselfish uprightness.

9. See John Hochman, M.D., "Miracle, Mystery and Authority: The Triangle of Cult Indoctrination," *Psychiatric Annals*, April 1990, http://www.rickross. com/reference/brainwashing/brainwashing 14.html

10. Fyodor Dostoyevsky, *The Brothers Karamazov* (New York, NY: Bantam Books, 1981 [originally published 1880]), p. 307; emphasis supplied.

11. From Hochman.

Chapter Four

The Day Love Died

*I*t starts with a sideways glance or two, accompanied by curiosity and admiration. Perhaps a conversation follows, and thoughts and feelings connect. By some strange, almost unconscious force, you find yourself gravitating toward another encounter, then another. A strange marvel unfolds. Pulse quickens and butterflies frolic whenever the two of you are in the same room. Little details about him or her register— the things they wear, the way they smell, a curve of the cheek. You talk, but on two levels: the conscious, rational level of concrete thoughts, and the unconscious, emotional level. A subliminal dance has begun. On some transcendent plane your souls are converging, coming to know one another as partners. Your outward behavior might remain composed, but the dam of your self-containment has broken and your affections are flooding the space between you and the one who has become their object. You begin to make special, consistent efforts to impress and please. You pray and hope they will be reciprocated. Somehow your ego is willing to lose itself in the approval of this one who has become your fascination. The birds sing sweeter, the sky is bluer, the stars are falling ... you are in love.

This preternatural experience is regarded by popular culture as the height of spiritual attainment. In its finest form, it graces the pages of great novels and beautifies the timeless legends of every society. In its raw form, it's sung about in pop songs, obsessed over in movies, plastered throughout magazines. It keeps the fashion industry throbbing as predictably as it keeps Hollywood in the black. And its power is understandable, as being in love is an exhilarating high. Yet the "self factor" in fallen human nature turns this phenomenon into a game of conquest. In most cases, falling in love is nothing more than an expression of the human ego. We fallen souls love those who bring us pleasure and benefit—when we find someone who delights our senses and emotions, we seek to acquire them in order to ensure ongoing happiness. To fix our affections upon the object of desire and then to seek to acquire reciprocal affections in order to enrich the self is, in essence, self-love.

Eros: The Gift Becomes God

The Bible presents God variously as our Friend, our Parent and our Lover. He who created the capacities for human affection is not above utilizing those channels to express the colors of His own all-encompassing love. Especially, sexual love, in the Greek *eros*, is a reflection of God's own intimate intentions toward His bride, the church. In its purity, marriage is a holy metaphor. Paul says, "Husbands, love your wives, just as Christ also loved the church, and gave Himself up for her" (Ephesians 5:25). In the Song of Solomon, God Himself takes the stage, speaking in the first person through Solomon: "Let us rise early and go to the vineyards; Let us see whether the vine has budded And its blossoms have opened, And whether the pomegranates have bloomed. There I will give you my love" (Song of Solomon 7:12). For God to unabashedly represent

His own love in such erotic terms is to give His most solemn blessing to this form of affection.

But sexual love is a strange, two-faced animal. Left to burn without boundaries, it becomes the most anti-God expression of all. In the heat of our fallen pursuits, we don't really love others; rather, we *use* them to love *ourselves*. The strongest evidence that sexual love is prone to be selfish love is found in the fact that the two have become identified in religious thought. Today philosophers and theologians say *eros* when they want to describe a love that is essentially selfish. Eros, in the theological arena, is a love that is prompted by the desirability of the object and bent upon acquiring that object for purposes of self-enrichment. The essential motivation in such a love is the pleasuring of self through bonding with another. This might be innocent enough, but because of the innate greed of fallen nature, the desire for sexual self-pleasure overrides care for others and for God. This sinful tendency corrupts eros completely. Apart from grace, our eros erodes into self-seeking, self-serving, and self-indulgence—thus the identification of sexual love with pure, unmingled selfishness.

Yet the prince of this world would mesmerize us into investing what is so often nothing but carnal lust with overtones of divinity. This has been his strategy since before the inception of Christianity. In Greek mythology, Eros was the son of Venus, the love goddess. According to legend, Eros was a handsome young man who was sent by the jealous Venus to cast a spell on the beautiful mortal Psyche. Eros instead fell in love with Psyche, which caused great conflict with his mother. Finally the conflict abated and Eros married Psyche, elevating her to divine status. The message in this myth is implicit: The soul, Psyche, is deified by sexual union. The trend of Greek thought continues to this day. The media presents the experience of sexual love as the greatest of all spiritual conquests, something that is charged with supernatural power. How many love songs say it will last "forever"?

Yet eros, left to wander outside of the Creator's constraints, turns out to be anything but divine and eternal. In the United States, nearly one out of two marriages ends in divorce. This statistic does not account for the non-married unions that end or the marriages that remain legally intact even while they are emotionally and spiritually fractured. If we take these factors into account, the attrition rate of eros relationships is much higher than 50 percent. This love that is invested with such expectations always seems to burn itself out after a brief span of time. Apart from the initial rush, it isn't so powerful after all.

This is where divine love, *agape,* comes in. Agape is the real thing, the foundational force that gives stability and longevity to all forms of human affection. Agape is the parent love that nurtures and disciplines all other loves. In a human relationship, agape supports the life of the relationship and keeps it from self-destruction the way a good mother both feeds and constrains her child. Agape is the perfect blend of grace and law, free gift and accountability, mercy and justice.

THE ORIGINAL LOVE AFFAIR

The Bible's first story dramatically proves the character of both kinds of love. After all, it's a story of a man and a woman who loved each other. Just *how* did they love each other, and with what *kind* of love? The answer to these questions changed with the introduction of sin. At Eden's dawn, their love was pure and holy, grounded in the selfless love of God. By the mysterious invasion of sin, however, the character of their love degraded into the self-love that characterizes fallen nature.

Eve "took of [the] fruit and ate. She also gave to her husband with her, and he ate" (Genesis 3:6 NKJV). Notice that Eve's first act after transgression was to seek connection to another. Social by nature, human beings want to share everything—including our sin. Suddenly "the eyes of both of them were opened," and as guilt and shame flooded over them, "they knew that they were naked." Attempting to smooth over the pangs of conscience, they fabricated flimsy garments of self-justification: "and they sewed fig leaves together, and made themselves loin coverings" (v. 7). When this cover-up scheme evaporated in the presence of a holy God, they sought to blame one another: "And the man said, 'The woman whom Thou gavest to be with me, she gave me from the tree, and I ate.' … And the woman said, 'The serpent deceived me, and I ate' " (vs. 12, 13). The man blamed the woman, the woman blamed the serpent, and both indirectly blamed God. Sin showed its true colors as human/divine and human/human relationships fractured into a billion brittle pieces.

It is truly astounding that Adam would scapegoat Eve. Realize that only hours before he had looked upon her gorgeous form and ached, *She has eaten of the tree, she's fallen. Now I have a choice. I can die with her, or live without her.* Out of "love" for Eve, he chose to die rather than separate from the beauty to which he had attached himself. When the full weight of his decision came to bear upon him, though, he experienced a change of heart. In the light of impending judgment, he tattled on her, hoping to escape condemnation himself. While only hours before Adam seemed ready to sacrifice himself for Eve, he now consigned her to divine retribution. Where was all the love he felt when she stood, all flushed and freshly fallen, with forbidden fruit in her hands?

Similarly, until the high wore off, Eve sought to "bless" Adam with the fruit that had seemed to so invigorate her. In her deluded state, she seemed more connected to Adam than ever. Then a powerfully dark psychic hangover led her to lose all connection to God and man. Desperately she flailed to deflect guilt from herself upon whomever she could find to absorb it. Where was the tender bond between herself and her spouse, between her soul and God?

While Adam's willingness to die with Eve might have mimicked love, we can be sure that it was not the real thing. True agape never puts another human before God. In eating the fruit, Adam actually catered to his own self-centered desire to be connected to someone for whom he felt deep affection. Because this love for his sinful wife was not tempered with hate for her sin, it became idolatry. He loved the sinner *and* the sin, and then he sinned himself. Likewise, Eve's "love" drew Adam into sin with her. Human affection became the kiss of death while it flowed wild, untempered by loyalty to God's law of love. Human affection, regardless of its divine origin and emotional richness, is just another expression of rebellion unless molded by principle and constrained by righteousness.

The end product of this affection gone out of bounds proved its nature. At first Adam was willing to die with, rather than live without, his wife. When the reality of that death sentence sank in, however, he suddenly detached from her and became willing to watch her die in his place! Thus she went from idol to scapegoat in the space of a few hours. He put her in place of God, and then he shoved her to the place of execution. Such is the instability of human affection apart from the constraining power of agape. First, we will exalt our loved one to replace God, and then when the consequences of our sin come, we will want them to replace us at the judgment seat!

And the height of arrogance is reached when the sovereign King is made to answer for the sin of those who rebel against Him. Our depraved impulse is to heap our soul's condemnation upon the head of God Himself. In shaming and blaming the blessed source of their only remaining hope, the guilty pair expressed human depravity at its most futile. In seeking to evade death, they further alienated themselves from the source of life.

JUSTICE AND MERCY, THE TWINS OF LOVE

In the saga of Eden's sin, we see the tension between the two sides of divine love. One side is affection for sinners— God's deep, passionate desire to be connected to the ones He adores. The other is hate for sin—heaven's perfect, holy repugnance of evil. Sin prompted Adam to lose the tension between these two pillars of love when he put affection for Eve above hatred for her sin. At that moment, and ever since, human love has been an unreliable indicator of the nature of divine love.

While the twin traits of affection for sinners and hate for sin ever existed in the character of God, they were forced into action by the appearance of transgression. Justice had no problem with sinless beings, nor did mercy have a mission in their behalf. Then with the debut of sin, agape divided its time between mercy and justice, alternately condemning sin and forgiving sinners. Mercy is the disposition to save the sinner. "*Save* me according to Your *mercy*" the psalmist prays, echoed by Paul's words, "according to His *mercy* He *saved* us" (Psalm 109:26; Titus 3:5 NKJV, emphasis supplied). Mercy mandates the salvation of souls. It is God's disposition to preserve, at any cost to Himself, the creatures of His hand. Then in perfect accord, hate for sin stands by mercy's side in the form of justice. It looks like this: "The wrath of God is revealed from heaven against all ungodliness and unrighteousness of men, who suppress the truth in unrighteousness" (Romans 1:18). The wrath is against ungodli*ness* and unrighteous*ness*. No personal vendettas or hit lists for the impartial One. His avowed enemy is sin itself, and His anger at sin is only released upon sinners as they cling to it. Yet it is part of His very nature to boil with fury toward the evil that wreaks havoc in His universe.

Normally we define love as synonymous with mercy and antonymous with justice:

Love = Mercy
Love ≠ Justice

A better formula presents justice and mercy as twin pillars of love:

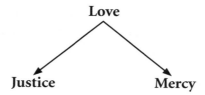

By marrying holy justice to sweet mercy, and keeping the two in perfect harmony within His divine person, God maintains the beautiful integrity of His character. This perfect balancing of justice and mercy requires absolute sympathy for sinners alongside absolute antipathy for sin. Because of sin, God's love is both positive and negative— positive toward sinners, whom He loves, and negative toward sin, which He hates. The same love that overflows with warm affection for created things must violently repulse that which would destroy those creatures and their habitat, and defy the law that upholds life itself. Hence the love that demands mercy toward God's children also demands justice toward the destroyer of His children. Sin blocks the channel whereby God's life-sustaining love can reach sinners. If God loves those beings that sin destroys, how can He not simultaneously hate that which destroys them? Just as intense as is His passion for souls is His anger toward that which suffocates them. God's love is a love that hates. To neuter it of destructive expressions in a sin-infested world is to rob it of vitality and virtue.

POSTMODERNISM LEADS MERCY ASTRAY

While love is a perfect balance of mercy and justice, we are prone to veer to one side or the other. Since the inception of postmodern thinking, which denies an absolute standard of righteousness and celebrates the power of the individual, we as a society have veered sharply to the left—affection for sinners apart from hate for sin. We celebrate the individual, and then drag the law of God, which is the only ultimate protector of the individual, in the dust. In our cultural enmity toward the law of God we see a rejection of the justice aspect of His love. The result is humanism, an exaltation of human beings and corresponding denigration of the supreme standard of righteousness. This can only lead to a sentimentalized, sensualized definition of love, such as we find permeating the media.

Film critic Michael Medved, commenting on the 2002 Oscars, pointed out that the underlying message of award-winning films is more often "follow your heart" than "do your duty." He said, "In recent years ... Do Your Duty has gone out of fashion. For instance, it's now considered part of conventional wisdom that it's better to follow your heart out of a marriage and into freedom or a new relationship rather than do your duty and stay in a partnership that has grown stale."[1] However, is this "follow your heart" formula really love? Can love divorced from duty sustain itself? The high mortality rate of relationships answers "no."

Rampant individualism, with its permissive "follow your heart" self-expression, has been accompanied by a deep antipathy for the law of God and its claims upon all people. These claims are seen as an unjust imposition and an unhealthy restraint. "Tolerance" is in style, but a form of tolerance that is, in the words of William Bennett, "a euphemism for moral exhaustion and a rigid or indifferent neutrality in response to every great moral issue."[2] G. K. Chesterton said this form of "tolerance" was "the virtue of people who do not believe in anything."[3] The effect of this exaltation of the individual and the corresponding disparagement of the law of God is the denigration of the principles of justice. Yet there is no real mercy without justice. Bennett puts his finger on the pulse of the problem when he says, "There is a vital link between reasonable judgment and authentic compassion."[4] And he echoes Benjamin Rush, who years before said, "The world stands in more need of justice than charity, and indeed it is the want of justice that renders charity everywhere so necessary."[5]

Modern Christianity, to the degree that it imbibes of the spirit of the world, has lost its hold on the justice side of love as well. The resulting definition of "love" is a sentimental, soft item that bears no resemblance to the original.

The love story of Eden is richer in emotional texture and pathos than any romance novel under the sun. All the elements of drama are there—the euphoria of new love, deep, passionate attachment, lust for power, intoxication, betrayal, and finally black despair. The story—as surreal as it might seem—is true, every word. This tragic garden is where we see the frailty of human love displayed alongside the perfection of God's agape. Selfish human love appears to possess great potency, but because it is not constrained by the great law of love, it burns itself to smoke and ashes. In contrast, divine love holds to both poles of mercy and justice, pouring itself out for all living creatures without compromising the law that sustains life. Amazingly, this love was not repelled by sin, but was rather driven by the emergency to new heights of expression, the highest being the cross of Jesus Christ.

Endnotes

1. Michael Medved, "When Will Hollywood Do Its Duty?" *U.S.A. Today,* March 15.

2. William Bennett, *The Death of Outrage* (New York: Simon & Schuster, 1999), p. 122.

3. As quoted in *The Death of Outrage*, p. 122.

4. *Ibid.*, p. 123.

5. Benjamin Rush, as quoted in *Our Sacred Honor*, ed. William Bennett (New York: Simon & Schuster, 1997), p. 313.

Chapter Five

Enter: The Lamb Slain

"Nowhere else is there to be found a revelation of Agape comparable to that in the death of Jesus on the Cross ... It testifies that it is a love that gives itself away, that sacrifices itself, even to the uttermost."
— Anders Nygren, *Agape and Eros* [1]

"The mystery of the cross explains all other mysteries. In the light that streams from Calvary the attributes of God which had filled us with fear and awe appear beautiful and attractive. Mercy, tenderness, and parental love are seen to blend with holiness, justice, and power."
— Ellen G. White, *The Great Controversy* [2]

THE PLACE OF THE SKULL

The human brain weighs about three pounds and looks like a large, pinkish-grey walnut. Its tissues are folded by various sulci, or grooves, that allow the 324 inches of surface area (about the size of a full newspaper, with each sheet spread out) of the brain to fit neatly into the skull. As with any functioning unit, the brain divides labor among its various branches, or lobes.

The frontal lobe is concerned with the "higher" functions of intellect; the parietal lobe deals in touch, temperature, and pain perception; the temporal lobe is for hearing and memory; and the occipital lobe, for vision. In addition to these lobes, the two hemispheres, right and left, have entirely different functions. The "military general" left half of the brain is involved in tasks such as logic, math and language. The "barefoot artist" right brain excels at spacial tasks, face recognition, visual imagery and music.

Without cooperative effort between the right and left hemispheres, the brain could not function well—for instance, we might recognize a face (right-brain function), but not be able to put a name with it (left-brain function). Fortunately, the Creator has planted an intermediary organ, called the *corpus callosum*, between the two worlds to join them together through its thick band of 200 to 250 million nerve fibers. Neurologist and 1981 Nobel Prize winner Roger Sperry, and neurologist Michael Gazzaniga, pioneered the "split brain" experiments that proved the specificity of the hemispheres' functions, and the problems that occur when they are severed from one another through the cutting of the corpus callosum.[3] While the subjects appeared to function normally, further testing revealed that they had difficulty coordinating right- and left-brain tasks, such as identifying articles that were placed in their hands, or building simple formations with blocks. Science has verified that we need that little bundle of nerve fibers to keep our brain from divorcing itself.

Reflecting our brain and its dependence upon the corpus callosum, the unaided human spirit is hopelessly divided against itself in its perception of reality. Truth always has two complementary aspects that on the surface seem contradictory, but in reality have a deep, underlying harmony. In grasping for truth, we fail to embrace its paradoxical nature and cleave to one side, ignoring or even despising the other. How many theological discussions, including the discussion of retributive justice, degenerate into a war between two opposing camps, with each camp holding to an element of truth while denying another? Most bad theology goes bad, not because it sets out to espouse error, but because it wars against some aspect of truth. How blind is human nature apart from divine infusion!

Truth itself is not to blame for the seeming disharmony. The deficiency is in the fallen mind. In discussing the subject of the covenants, Paul makes this observation of the unbelieving Jews who could not see the fullness of new covenant truth:

> "But their minds were hardened; for until this very day at the reading of the old covenant the same veil remains unlifted, because it is removed in Christ. But to this day whenever Moses is read, a veil lies over their heart" (2 Corinthians 3:14, 15).

The hardness that comes over the conscience that is not made supple by the Holy Spirit is identified as a "veil" that lies over the heart. Blind to the new covenant of grace, which built upon but did not deny the claims of the Old Testament law, the Jews groped in the spiritual darkness of incomplete knowledge and circumscribed experience. In their groping we see the human condition—our minds are veiled and unable to see the glory, or character, of God. But there is hope for the blind among us in the simple words "It is removed in Christ." Embrace Jesus Christ, Paul says, and the veil is lifted.

More specifically, Paul states, "Whenever a man turns to the Lord, the veil is taken away" (v. 16). "Lord" is from the Greek *Kurios*, which means "one who wields authority for good." In this definition, the interrelationship between the justice and mercy "hemispheres" of God's love is stated simply. In justice, God upholds His law in the universe. He does it, however, not as a self-centered authoritarian, but "for good"—in mercy to His creatures. This interdependency of the twin attributes of God is what is seen when the veil is lifted from our eyes.

Since the veil was literally removed, or torn, at the moment Jesus died,[4] and since the cross of Christ is the apex of the expression of His character, we can safely conclude that the contemplation of the cross is the best way to sharpen our own vision of the nature of love. When human pride is deflated, nothing rises up to block truth from our hearts. The awareness of heaven's great sacrifice stills the soul in God's molding hand. Miraculously, the supporting poles of justice and mercy are seen to uphold the love of all loves. The heart is dignified by justice, melted by mercy, and finally transformed by agape.

This sublime reality was diagramed by a divine hand at the scene of the cross itself. The Gospel writers identify Golgotha as "the place of the skull."[5] Likewise, Calvary is *kranion* in Greek, similar to our "cranium," and also means "skull."[6] Many scholars agree that the hill upon which Jesus was crucified was a knoll shaped like a hairless human head.[7] And there in the middle of the "skull" Jesus was providentially lifted up, as if to tell us that a hopelessly shattered human "kranion" can be healed through the contemplation of His selfless death. Our thought patterns, naturally at enmity with one aspect of God or another, can be set aright through communion with the dying Lamb, until finally we surrender to all the fullness of who He is.

MADE A CURSE FOR US

While we fail to embrace the harmony of God's character, our innate turbulence soon finds its way into the relational realm. Apart from agape, our personal unions are doomed to degenerate into a war of the wills. When Adam and Eve lost their connection to God, they immediately felt the effects in their relationship to one another. But into the midst of the world's first marital dispute God asserted Himself, giving the first Messianic promise recorded in the Bible. "I will put enmity Between [the serpent] and the woman, And between your seed and her seed; He shall bruise you on the head, And you shall bruise him on the heel" (Genesis 3:15). A divinely originated opposition to sin would be placed in the heart of the woman as she received salvation from sin. The source of this salvation would be found in the "seed" of the woman. This seed would mortally wound the serpent by "bruising," or literally crushing, his head.

This seed was the promised Messiah, the "Lamb slain from the foundation of the world" (Revelation 13:8 KJV). God's Son would sacrifice Himself for the salvation of humanity. Because God is not limited by time, the cross was an immediate reality to Him even though it had yet to be witnessed by us. His promises are so irrevocably sure that His plan to perform an action instantly avails the benefits of that action. Heaven's ruling that Christ should die, immediately reversed corporate humanity's sentence of condemnation and granted us the undeserved gift of life.[8]

Arriving at this decision, however, was a slow, agonizing process for the triune God. Sin presented a problem of gigantic proportions to the sinless One. Divine holiness could not be compromised in order to access degraded mankind, but compassion could not help but yearn for its wandering children. In solemn alarm, the Godhead locked itself into extended negotiations, until finally the "counsel of peace" was formed between the "two offices" of justice and mercy— the pact would meet the demands of both (Zechariah 6:13). Christ would come in human form, and then as our Advocate live in perfect righteousness. He would then offer that life up in a death that would deplete mankind's death penalty.[9] The demands of both justice and mercy would be satisfied in the living and dying of the Savior. "Lovingkindness and truth have met together; Righteousness and peace have kissed each other" (Psalm 85:10).

Since the law was as holy as God Himself, only one equal with the law could atone for its transgression. Christ was divine. The law also demanded that the very one who harbored sin would die, for the purpose of the law's death penalty was not to vent some arbitrary rage, but to destroy the infection of sin before it spread. Justice could allow for no substitutes, but mandated that "*the soul who sins* will die" (Ezekiel 18:4, emphasis supplied). In order to qualify as the sacrificial Lamb, Jesus must so closely identify with the human race in its sin that His death could righteously be counted as our own. This God accomplished by "sending His own Son in the likeness of sinful flesh and as an offering for sin," with the result that "He condemned sin in the flesh, in order that the requirement of the Law might be fulfilled in us, who do not walk according to the flesh, but according to the Spirit" (Romans 8:3, 4).

The death that successfully condemned sin in the flesh is known in the Scriptures as the "curse of the law." "Christ redeemed us from the curse of the Law, having become a curse for us—for it is written, 'Cursed is everyone who hangs on a tree'" (Galatians 3:13). This curse was understood by God's people to be the result of transgression. As the children of Israel stood poised for the invasion of Canaan, Moses rehearsed the law, saying, "Cursed is he who does not confirm the words of this law by doing them" (Deuteronomy 27:26). Failure to obey the law in every particular brings the soul under the law's cloud of condemnation—for the law that upholds the harmony of the universe cannot permit sin's discord. This curse demands the utter annihilation of the one who has become a host for the parasite of sin.

This phenomenon is called the "second death," because for those who are eternally lost, it occurs after a physical death and subsequent resurrection.[10] It will be a time when souls meet the full ramifications of their love of sin and their rejection of the Savior. There are two aspects to this second death: an encounter with God's unmingled justice in the form of His wrath against sin, and the utter withdrawal of God's mercy from the individual personality. It can be said that God's full judgment against sin is a thing of both substance and space—substance in the form of consuming fire against cherished sin, space in the form of personal abandonment. Jesus Himself often presented this twofold picture of final punishment before He went on to endure it in our behalf.[11]

As we live our lives today, God withholds the death-dealing impact of His justice and reaches forth with undeserved mercy. He restrains His integral anger at our sin, even while sustaining and blessing us. There will be a day when the situation will be fearfully reversed. Pure, unmingled indignation against sin will pour forth from His presence, while individual persons will be disengaged from the source of their existence. But this need never be. Jesus Himself wrung out the ravages of fiery substance and lonely space in our behalf when God "made Him who knew no sin to be sin on our behalf" (2 Corinthians 5:21). While never participating in sin, Jesus saddled Himself to its crushing weight and took its divinely ordained penalty. Through faith in Him, we can have sin consumed out of our hearts by the holy fire of His love. This faith looks at the great gift of the cross in grateful awe. There our Jesus endured an experience that we will never know fully, but will ever strive to understand.

FIERY SUBSTANCE

"Clouds and thick darkness surround Him; Righteousness and justice are the foundation of His throne. Fire goes before Him, And burns up His adversaries round about" (Psalm 97:2, 3). The righteousness and justice of God are manifest in the "fire" of God's presence, which is mentioned in Scripture more than 150 times.[12] Sinless beings do not fear this phenomenon. Before his fall Lucifer "walked up and down in the stones of fire." A glorified Elijah was taken to heaven in a burning chariot. God's purified people will finally walk on the "sea of glass mingled with fire."[13] This fire is designed to consume the grime of sin from whatever it confronts. Sinless beings have nothing to fear from it, but when a soul is fully identified with sin, God's raging holiness will consume the soul itself. Not through His own sin, but by assuming ours, Jesus embraced a position of full association with that which provokes the fire of God's wrath. Thus He subjected Himself to the soul-melting phenomenon expressed in the words, "Thy wrath has rested upon me. ... Thy burning anger has passed over me" (Psalm 88:7, 16).

No literal fire came from heaven to consume Jesus upon the cross, because no encounter with an external manifestation of God's holiness was necessary. Jesus *was* the manifestation of God's holiness, the "radiance of His glory and the exact representation of His nature" (Hebrews 1:3). Within His own breast He bore the sin-consuming Shekinah. Thus a strange, violent combination of forces occurred within the person of Jesus when this holy fire shared a space with sin itself. Jesus felt the concurrence of His Father with the witness of His own inner Shekinah's condemnation of sin, which He had become in our behalf. The two opposing forces of sin and holiness collided within the core of the sinless One, bringing a psychological conflict so severe that His heart literally exploded in grief.[14]

GOD-FORSAKEN SPACE

Encapsulated in fallen humanity, Jesus went to His cross to bear unspeakable loneliness in our stead. Ray by ray, the flood of God's approbation was removed from Him. A holy God could not look upon even His own Son once He had become burdened with the sin of the world. The Father and the Son, ever bonded in love, began to feel the mutual horror of separation. Like earthly parents releasing their child to a terminal illness, but a billion times more, the Father felt the tearing out of His holy affections. Like a boy drowning in a dark sea, feeling forgotten by the one who had always protected him, Jesus' soul was broken on the rocks of unrequited love.

None of us fully realizes the degree to which we depend upon the evidence of God's love for us—the deep, inner support that comes from the ongoing sustenance of life. Let that life be withdrawn, and our beings will feel what it is to lose God. Lost souls are like turbulent, rebellious children who maintain a hostile dependency upon their Creator and Redeemer, ever ungrateful for His love, but unaware of their total dependency upon it. How deceived we are to live in revolt against the One who is responsible for every breath we take, every morsel of food we eat, and every ounce of pleasure we enjoy. When choice is finally and fully honored, and God withdraws His presence from those who have continually spurned it, a horror will come over lost souls that will produce "weeping and gnashing of teeth" such as has never been heard.[15]

But when the golden light of heaven's approval was shunted from the soul of Christ, it was from One who had ever returned glory to God, who had lived in gratitude for the evidences of His love. Not because of His own sin, but ours, Jesus experienced being cut off from the source of life, and the breaking of His heart as He felt the cold doom of divine abhorrence. Of all the tortures He endured, this was the greatest. He could bear anything if He knew His Father loved Him, but in the darkness of Calvary, even God was gone. "My God, My God, why hast Thou forsaken Me?" He cried (Matthew 27:46).

Who Killed Jesus?

So who killed Jesus? The Romans? The Jews? The devil? How about God Himself? While all of these entities played a part in the death of Christ, none of them actually took His life, for He *gave* it of His own accord. While our lives are not our own, Jesus' life belonged to Him, unborrowed, underived. No one could take it from Him without His consent. His trickling blood was drawn forth by hands that He sustained, and so in essence it was poured out by Him. Simply put, He "gave Himself" (Galatians 1:4; 1 Timothy 2:6; Titus 2:14). This pouring-out motion is the essential movement of agape, which, rather than reaching up to enrich self, reaches down to save others. The red river that spattered the rock of Golgotha was evidence of the pouring out of saving love upon the head of every man, woman and child, for "All flesh shall see the salvation of God" (Luke 3:6).

In perfect sync with the downward sweeping of Christ's condescension was the movement of the Father in giving His Son. Dearer to Him than His own life, Jesus represented all the riches of heaven itself. Wrapped up in the gift of Christ was irrefutable evidence that there was *nothing* God would withhold from us. If He would give Christ, He would give anything. "He who did not spare His own Son, but delivered Him up for us all, how will He not also with Him freely give us all things?" (Romans 8:32).

If God gives all things, then why does He at last take life away from those who are unworthy of it? Numerous accounts clearly depict God's participation in the destruction of the wicked.[16] Can we then fault God in the death of the wicked? Not ultimately. A child can logically follow the reasoning that if God freely *gave* the gift of life when He *gave* His Son, then the reason some finally *lose* life is because they would not receive God's gift. It was not a reluctance to give on God's part, but their own unwillingness to receive His gift, which places the lost in the throes of death.

In the end, God's wrath against sin follows the same path as did His agape. It will be "mixed in full strength" and "poured out"[17] upon those who leave no other option. But can we fault God for unleashing this wrath, which is an expression of the holiness of His love, when He first absorbed it into Himself?

Can we impugn God's love, adding Him to the terrorist lineup in the Hall of Blame, simply because He destroys those who would not receive the life He gave at infinite sacrifice? Which of the Osama Bin Ladens of the world first gave themselves to save those they finally destroyed?

The severity of divine retribution has caused many to question God's love. As a result, some explain away the judgments of God, others reject God altogether. Still others embrace divine retribution while cherishing a vindictive, harsh picture of God. There is a better option than all of these. We can look to the hill Golgotha, where Jesus gave Himself, and allow the veil of confusion and imbalance to be lifted from our eyes. Then we will trust Him even in His most punitive moments. Seeing divine judgment through the prism of the cross proves even God's wrath to be organic to His love, for His wrath goes nowhere that His love didn't go first, and destroys no one whom He didn't first die to save.

Endnotes

1. Anders Nygren, *Agape and Eros* (Chicago: University of Chicago Press, 1982), p. 118.

2. Ellen G. White, *The Great Controversy* (Mountain View, CA: Pacific Press Publishing Association, 1950), p. 652.

3. "A Science Odyssey" http://www.pbs.org/wgbh/aso/databank/entries/bhsper.html

4. See Matthew 27:50, 51.

5. See Matthew 27:33; Mark 15:22; John 19:17.

6. Greek Lexicon from *Strong's Exhaustive Concordance of the Bible*, Hendrickson Publishers, entry 2898, for the word "Calvary."

7. See, for instance, the *Catholic Encyclopedia* "Golgotha" entry at http://www.newadvent.org/cathen/03191a.htm

8. See Romans 5:16–18.

9. Hebrews 2:14–18; Philippians 2:5–8; Romans 8:3–5.

10. Hebrews 9:27; also Revelation 2:11; 20:6, 14; 21:8.

11. In Jesus' teachings on final punishment, He sometimes speaks of the fate of the wicked as fire, and sometimes as outer darkness. See Matthew 3:12; 7:19, 23; 8:12; 13:41–42, 49–50; 18:8, 9; 25:29, 30; Luke 3:17.

12. Research done through "The Unbound Bible,"
http://www.theunboundbible.org

13. See Ezekiel 28:14; 2 Kings 2:11; Revelation 15:2.

14. See John 19:34.

15. See, for instance, Matthew 25:29, 30.

16. See Chapter Eighteen.

17. Revelation 14:10; 16:1.

The Judge of All the Earth

ough hands grab His beaten form and thrust Him onto the waiting cross. Deftly, they jerk His unresisting arms into an open embrace and fix them there for the remainder of His life. Nailing His feet, they lift Him heavenward and violently jolt His cross into the earth. Bearing all that, and their sins as well, Christ can only breathe in behalf of His tormentors, "Father, forgive them; for they know not what they do" (Luke 23:34 KJV).

Yet some day soon this Prince of Forgiveness will return and resurrect many of those same tormentors for whom He so tenderly prayed.[1] And when He does, the force of His displeasure toward them will be so palpable that they will try desperately to hide "themselves in the caves and in the rocks of the mountains," and will say "to the mountains and rocks, 'Fall on us and hide us from the face of Him who sits on the throne and from the wrath of the Lamb! For the great day of His wrath has come, and who is able to stand?'" (Revelation 6:15–17).

What happened to the love? What happened to the tender mercy? How to harmonize the endearing image of the forgiving Lamb slain with that of the apocalyptic avenging judge? For that matter, how do we retrospectively reconcile this loving Lamb with the seemingly unsparing Old Testament Judge who instructed Israel to "utterly destroy" every man, woman and child in the Promised Land into which He was sending them (Deuteronomy 20:17)?

It would seem that the Lamb slain of our last chapter is a far cry from this avenging "Judge of all the earth" (Genesis 18:25). Yet God is not schizophrenic. All of His apparently irreconcilable attributes spring from an internally consistent character that is "the same yesterday, today and forever" (Hebrews 13:8). And that character, as we've discovered, is best conceptualized through the clarifying lens of the cross, where justice and mercy met and made peace, where God's self-sacrificing agape is seen to be the motive for all His actions.

When we examine the inspired record of God's judicial interventions through this cross-etched lens, we no longer see the classic caricature of a fire-breathing tyrant who seizes on every excuse to destroy His own creation. We see a grieving Creator reluctantly sweeping away in the Flood the morally unsalvageable many to save the viable few, that He might preserve the world long enough to receive its Messiah. We see a Savior delivering a helpless nation of slaves, and all who would join them, from the oppressive power of idolatry, that He might adopt them as the "children" through whom that Messiah will come. We see a long-suffering Father agonizing over how to give up these persistently wayward children, whose determined perversity prevents Him from shielding them from their powerful Assyrian and Babylonian neighbors. We see life-giving mercy implied in these, and all of God's judicial acts, as He intervenes to vindicate the (relatively) innocent and punish the unrepentant guilty[2], to spare the latter from adding to their guilt and condemnation, and to spare the former from being further subjected to their destructive influence.

With our agape glasses firmly in place, and God's benevolent character as our point of reference, we can most accurately survey the full spectrum of divine retribution as portrayed in the Old Testament. Let's begin by dispelling some entrenched myths about how God "does" judgment.

A COMPLEX INTERPLAY

Divine judgment is an infinitely complex process that involves principles and variables that we, with our fallen minds, can only begin to grasp. In our efforts to understand it, we've tended to oversimplify it. Depending on our personal experience, temperamental bias and religious background (or lack of it), we tend to regard judgment as residing at either the right or left extreme of the theological-philosophical spectrum. In so doing, we buy into and propagate some classic, faith-destroying myths.

Myth #1: God sovereignly predestines and imposes judgment without regard to the human agent. Residing at the extreme right of the judgment spectrum is the Calvinistic perception that, in the words of a contemporary apologist:

> "The will of God is inevitable. God does what He wants."[3] "Should God have created all men for no other purpose than to consign them to an eternity in hell … we would have no recourse. There would be no reason to protest. God can do with that which is His own *as He wishes*. … You were made to glorify Him either as a vessel of mercy or as a vessel of wrath."[4]

Coupled with this assertion of arbitrary predestination and divine unaccountability is the idea that God micro-manages the minutest affairs of life:

"We are dealing with a God of detail. He is great enough to concern Himself with every detail in all of the universe. It is a small God who bothers only with ends while caring nothing about means. [The] details of divine predestination nicely accord with [such actions as] the opening of a door and the moves in a chess game."[5]

While such a view of divine sovereignty professes to factor in human free will, one is hard pressed to see where it practically fits into the picture. If God predetermines some to be objects of His wrath, and micro-manages the affairs of their lives to facilitate this—and is ultimately unaccountable to them or anyone else for these machinations—the whole concept of free choice is, for all practical purposes, nullified. It's not hard to see why such a skewed conception of divine wrath and judgment sends so many fleeing to the opposite extreme of the spectrum.

Myth #2: God never intervenes to punish or protect, nor does He guarantee a just conclusion to this life. "Macho God" overkill tends to have a backlash effect, causing us to recoil into the arms of its temperamental inverse—a safe and warm but rather impotent God who is held captive by chaos and His own laws of nature. In his 1981 bestseller, *When Bad Things Happen to Good People*, Rabbi Harold Kushner envisions such a God:

"God wants the righteous to live peaceful, happy lives, but sometimes even He can't bring that about. It is too difficult even for God to keep cruelty and chaos from claiming their innocent victims."[6]

"No matter what stories we were taught about Daniel or Jonah in Sunday School, God does not reach down to interrupt the workings of laws of nature to protect the righteous from harm." [7]

While it's one thing to observe that God most often works within the parameters of His established natural laws of cause and effect, it's quite another to contradict the Scriptures and forbid Him to manage His creation as He knows best. And while we can honestly conclude that He has, with some notable exceptions, chosen the path of least intrusion out of deference for the principles at stake in the cosmic conflict between good and evil, we undermine His divinity if we cite inherent weakness as the source of His tolerance of evil. Even so, we might be able to resign ourselves to a temporarily non-intrusive God if we could be assured that He will at some point step in to soundly defeat entrenched wickedness. But like the God he conceptualizes, Kushner is able to empathize with our plight but can offer no absolute assurance:

"Sometimes, because our souls yearn for justice, because we so desperately want to believe that God will be fair to us, we fasten our hopes on the idea that life in this world is not the only reality. Somewhere beyond this life is another world where 'the last shall be first' and those whose lives were cut short here on earth will be reunited with those they loved, and will spend eternity with them. Neither I nor any other living person can know anything about the reality of that hope ... since we cannot know for sure, we would be well advised to take this world as seriously as we can, in case it turns out to be the only one we'll ever have, and to look for justice and meaning here." [8]

Will the real judge please stand up? If God is not a hard-boiled, megalomaniacal prosecuting attorney who always gets His man or an empathetic but virtually impotent public defender, then how does He "do" judgment? What kind of judge is He? As ever, the truth lies somewhere between and outside of the polarizing extremes of human exaggeration and oversimplification.

Our paradoxical God is both sovereign and flexible, both independent and interactive, both authoritative and approachable.[9] While He is the great initiator in His cosmic conversation with humanity, He is also proactively responsive to human input. At once immanent and transcendent, with all and over all, He overcomes evil in the lives of those who are willing and overrules it in the lives of those who are not. He is "the Alpha and the Omega, the Beginning and the End," the divine parentheses around the human experience (Revelation 1:8). What He sovereignly initiated through creation and redemption, He will perfectly conclude with judgment, framing our lives with the force and inevitability of truth, yet leaving us free to identify with or deny it.

This means that, while His will cannot fail of fulfillment in the overruling, overarching sense, it can certainly be frustrated in its most intimate and personal application. For what is the will of God? What does He want more than anything else? He "desires *all* men to be saved and to come to the knowledge of the truth" (1 Timothy 2:4, emphasis supplied). "The Lord is ... not willing that *any* should perish but that *all* should come to repentance" (2 Peter 3:9, emphasis supplied).

This is precisely why judgment is both necessary and defensible. If God has predestined some to be saved and the rest to be lost, and deprives the latter of His saving, enabling grace, He has no right to punish them for their moral failures and crimes. Moral accountability implies an appropriate framework within which we are given the skills, tools and motivation to become moral people. This framework is provided by the compelling, empowering logic of the cross. Because Christ has given His life for the life of our lost world, and has suffused it with an atmosphere of saving, enabling grace that is as real and free and vital as the air we breathe, we are without excuse if we choose to persist in the path of rebellion. According to our privileges will be our accountability.

And so the divine Judge enters into a complex interplay of give-and-take, of call-and-response, as He interacts with fallen humanity. Sometimes spectacularly, but usually without fanfare, He judges evil by overcoming, overturning and overruling it for and with good. He illustrated this reassuring truth to Ezekiel in his vision of the cherubim and the wheels within the wheels.[10] As the intricately interconnected wheels operated under the guidance of the divine hand that supported the wings of the cherubim, and over all was the throne of God, so the divine mind oversees and participates in the complexity of human events, while ever respecting the freedom of choice that He Himself has established. It's a flexible approach that results in a variety of judicial interventions ranging from the imperceptible to the dramatically intrusive. Add to this variety the element of apparent contradiction, and the biblical picture can become quite challenging.

THE INTRINSIC-EXTRINSIC CONTINUUM

For instance, God says of apostatizing Israel, in one breath, "Behold, the eyes of the Lord God are upon the sinful kingdom, and *I will destroy it* from off the face of the earth," and in the next, "O Israel, *thou hast destroyed thyself;* but in me is thine help (Amos 9:8; Hosea 13:9 KJV, emphasis supplied). And again, God says of rebellious Judah, all in the same breath, "*I will deliver* [you] ... into the hand of Nebuchadnezzar king of Babylon," and "*I Myself will fight against you* with an outstretched hand ... *I will strike* the inhabitants of this city" (Jeremiah 21:7, 5, 6, emphasis supplied).[11] Now which is it? Did God destroy Israel or did they destroy themselves? Did God simply give Judah up to the tragic consequences of their sinful choices, or did He actually enable a heathen nation to violently subdue them? And could it be that all of these things happened at once?

Because the face of divine judgment is so multifaceted, we've found it helpful to picture its varied expressions plotted on a continuum that ranges from the intrinsic, meaning that which belongs to or arises from within one's very nature, to the extrinsic, meaning that which is externally imposed. And because that same face is so comprehensive as to seem, at times, contradictory, we've found that the same judgment event can plot in a variety of places at once. It's all very challenging to our limited spiritual perceptions, yet how could we expect less from a divine being whose essential agape nature is a marriage of seemingly contradictory characteristics?

While we'll delve more deeply into the "intrinsic-extrinsic continuum" idea in the chapters following, for the sake of clarity and continuity we've included a brief summary here, beginning with a diagram:

Divine Retributive Justice				
Intrinsic				Extrinsic
Intrinsic Justice	Divine "Giving Up"	Judgment Through Hostile Human Agencies	Judgment Through Cooperative Human Agencies	Direct Divine Intervention

Intrinsic justice: Because God has designed, and continually sustains, creation to operate according to life-giving laws that reflect His beneficent character, negative natural consequences result when these laws are violated.

These consequences reveal the innate destructiveness of sin, which at its heart is really anarchy, or anti-law. This is the primary sense in which apostatizing Israel "destroyed itself"— it literally brought destruction into and upon itself by making life-destroying choices—it, in essence, acted suicidally.

Yet this concrete outworking of intrinsic justice does more than reveal the innate destructiveness of sin. Because God has made the natural to foreshadow the spiritual, it implies a *moral* dimension to rebellion, with extrinsic judicial consequences: "For since the creation of the world [God's] invisible attributes are clearly seen, being understood by the things that are made, even His eternal power and Godhead, so that [those who suppress the truth] are without excuse" (Romans 1:20). In this way, intrinsic justice also reveals the divine disapproval of, and inability to indefinitely sustain, those who flagrantly indulge in destructive choices and behaviors. This is the secondary sense in which Israel is said to have "destroyed itself"—they were morally responsible for making the choices that forced God to impose judicial consequences upon them, for their own sakes, and for the greater good.

Divine "giving up": As He regards those who persistently "suppress the truth" and reject His redemptive overtures, God says, "My Spirit shall not strive [or abide] with man forever" (Romans 1:18; Genesis 6:3). Because receiving God's Holy Spirit is a privilege to which we must consent, He can't and won't force Himself into the minds and lives of those who refuse Him. As He is persistently rebuffed, He must withdraw His enlightening Spirit; and when He is firmly and finally rejected, He must abandon the intransigent to wander in the darkness they have chosen. This divine withdrawal and abandonment is the next step on the judgment continuum.

"Although [the incorrigibly resistant] knew God, they did not glorify Him as God, nor were thankful, but became futile in their thoughts, and their foolish hearts were darkened. ... Therefore God also gave them up" (Romans 1:21, 24).

To what did, and does, God "give them up"? To the further destruction of their own characters and lives, to demonic oppression and possession, to the aggressive actions of the people and nations around them. It is in this sense that God reluctantly removed His protective hedge and "delivered," or gave Judah up, to their Babylonian conquerors.

Judgment through hostile human agencies: While God removes His protective hedge from those who have forced Him out of their lives, He does more than passively "give them up" to the inevitable consequences they have brought upon themselves. As their moral intransigence translates into immoral and oppressive behavior, He also delivers them up to extrinsic judgment—correctively, if they will receive it as such—punitively, if they will not. In a sense, He hands them over from one part of Himself to another, from the advocate to the judge. It's in this capacity that He actively authorized and enabled Babylon to subdue Judah. He describes the granting of this "punishing power" to Babylon in unmistakably clear and strong language, "A sword is sharpened and Also polished ... To be given into the hand of the slayer" (Ezekiel 21:9, 11).

Yet contradictory as it may seem, God did not inspire their hostility. It arose from within their carnal hearts, but He overruled it for purposes of judgment. As He said of Assyria, whom He employed as His "rod of anger," "I send him against a godless nation, I dispatch him against a people who anger me. ... But this is not what *he* intends, this is not what *he* has in mind; his purpose is to destroy, to put an end to many nations" (Isaiah 10:6, 7 NIV, emphasis supplied). This, of course, is not a perfect revelation of divine justice, compromised as it is by carnal cruelty and passion. Yet God identifies Himself as making use of it as He condescends to work within the constricting parameters of human perversity.

Judgment through cooperative human agencies: Yet more explicit and unambiguous is God's execution of justice through cooperative human agencies. This is the kind of straightforward judgment we see meted out within and through the nation of Israel, who, as a divinely established theocracy, sustained a unique relationship to God. Having voluntarily entered into covenant relationship with the Judge of all the earth, they consented to place themselves under His direct discipline. This means that, far from being objects of divine favoritism, they were held to an even more rigorous moral standard than their unbelieving neighbors, insofar as they were the recipients and repositories of greater light.

Yet as ideal as it may sound, and much as contemporary Christianity might romanticize it, this theocratic relationship never matured into its full, divinely intended potential. God yearned to "make a new covenant with the house of Israel ... not according to the covenant that [He] made with their fathers ... which they broke" (Jeremiah 31:31, 32). He lovingly labored to take them beyond the system of punishments and rewards through which He condescended to relate to them in their spiritual infancy. But His best efforts to "put [His] law in their minds, and write it on their hearts" were, more often than not, rebuffed (v. 33). Though this theocratic relationship will never be duplicated prior to the second coming, God's ideal of a spiritually mature people who understand and practice the core principles of righteousness and cooperative judgment will finally be realized in spiritual Israel.[12]

Direct divine intervention: The least ambiguous and most explicitly extrinsic of all the types of judgment is that delivered directly from the hand of God, either through the miraculous manipulation of natural forces or through angelic agencies. We aren't left to wonder, for instance, who orchestrated the worldwide Flood: "The Lord saw that the wickedness of man was great in the earth, and that every intent of the thoughts of his heart was only evil continually. ... So the Lord said, '*I will destroy* man whom I have created from the face of the earth' " (Genesis 6:5, 7, emphasis supplied). In identifying God as the source of this and other catastrophic judgments, such as those imposed against Sodom and Gomorrah, and Egypt in the time of the Exodus, the Bible is unambiguous and unapologetic. Though He is "grieved in His heart" to "bring to pass ... His unusual act" of destruction, God must rise to the occasion and intervene for the greater good (Genesis 6:6; Isaiah 28:21).

Yet even in such instances of severe retributive justice, mercy is not abandoned. Ample opportunity and motivation for repentance are provided, and those willing to separate themselves from sin are given a way of escape. And while such judgments would appear to be unilaterally conceived, the biblical context often either implies or explicitly reveals human cooperation, both as an "outcry against" the sin and as intercessory prayer in behalf of the sinners[13] (Genesis 18:20). And above and beyond all the complex concerns and the dizzying details, such decisive interventions assure us that God really does care, He really is in control, and justice will ultimately prevail.

A SOLID FOUNDATION

No doubt, this brief summary has raised some questions even while answering others. We'll do our best to address those questions in the following chapters, where we'll delve more deeply into the intrinsic-extrinsic continuum concepts, in the context of the Old Testament chronology. But for now, we've established a foundation. We know that while God is sovereign, He is ever sensitive to human input and freedom of choice. We know that His ability to bring about justice is so creative and comprehensive that He can work both because of, and in spite of, the human agent, though it's ever His preference to win our cooperation. We know that He imposes judgment in a variety of ways—through the laws of nature and our very beings, through human and angelic agencies, through miraculous manipulation of the forces of nature.

Moreover, we know that, whatever avenue He chooses to work through, and however severe may be its expression, His justice always proceeds from His unselfish love. "The Judge of all the earth" will ever and always be "the Lamb slain from the foundation of the world," as His eternal scars will testify.

Endnotes

1. See Matthew 26:64; Revelation 1:7.

2. It's worth noting that "punish" does not equate to "torture." Just punishment involves the appropriate meting out, from a source of moral authority, of pain, loss or suffering for a crime or wrongdoing. Torture is the gratuitous inflicting of physical or emotional pain for purely sadistic reasons. While God never tortures, He unashamedly claims responsibility for imposing punishment where it is due.

3. Jay Adams, *The Grand Demonstration* (Santa Barbara, CA: EastGate Publishers, 1991), p. 55.

4. *Ibid.*, pp. 49, 50, emphasis in original.

5. *Ibid.*, p. 57.

6. Harold S. Kushner, *When Bad Things Happen to Good People* (New York: Quill, 2001), p. 43. While Kushner's book is to be commended for its warmth, candor, and many practical insights, his view of God's nature and sovereignty is at odds with the biblical record.

7. *Ibid.*, p. 58.

8. *Ibid.*, pp. 28, 29.

9. In conceptualizing God's paradoxical nature, we must be careful not to mistakenly conclude that He is composed of truly contradictory, mutually exclusive characteristics, such as "eternal and temporal," "immutable and ever-evolving," etc. Though His character is so comprehensive and multifaceted as to, at times, appear contradictory to us, He is ever consistent within Himself.

10. See Ezekiel 1 and 10.

11. During the reign of Solomon's son, Rehoboam, 10 tribes broke away from the monarchy to form the Northern Kingdom of Israel; the two remaining tribes, Judah and Benjamin, became the Southern Kingdom of Judah.

12. See Chapter Twelve.

13. See, for instance, Genesis 18:16–33; 19:13; Exodus 2:23–25.

Chapter Seven

Satan, the Instigator ... God, the Accomplice?

The biblical world-view is the only one that accepts the reality of evil and suffering while giving both the cause and the purpose, while offering God-given strength and sustenance in the midst of it. Those who refuse to accept these truths that Jesus presents will continue to find this a barrier to God and, I dare suggest, a barrier to reason itself." —Ravi Zacharias, *Jesus Among Other Gods*[1]

INNOCENT SUFFERING

No probing into the subject of the judgment is complete without an elucidation of the origin and workings of evil. We have discussed the fall of Lucifer and the fall of humankind. We know that evil exists in our cosmos because of these things. Judgment is God's response to that evil, and the subject of this book. Before we enter into a detailed study of God's judgments, though, we need to establish the reality that God's enemy counterfeits those judgments.

Imagine that your beloved son is diagnosed with a genetic condition called *progeria*. As a result of the disease, he will age roughly ten times faster than a normal child—meaning that at seven, his body will groan under the same infirmities as a 70-year-old body. His growth will halt before he reaches four feet tall. When his cheeks should be fat, pink apples, they will dissolve into bony hollows. His forehead and mouth will be framed with wrinkles; his bald head will never grow hair. His joints will stiffen; his blood will thicken with fat. Rather than worrying about him riding his bike in the street, you will worry about hip dislocations and heart attacks, strokes and arthritis—because he will be, biologically speaking, much older than you.

While your agony over his disease marks your every moment, you feel a deeper ache than even the encroachments of death can bring. It stems from the fact that only one in eight million are reported to have this disease.[2] Its sheer rarity rubs the wound with the sense of being singled out for punishment. What great sin did you commit that fate's finger—or perhaps God's—should point to you?

This is the emotional turmoil that wracked the life of Rabbi Harold Kushner when his son, Aaron, was diagnosed with progeria. Like so many of us, he cherished the notion that suffering comes as a punishment for wrongdoing, that "tragedies like this were supposed to happen to selfish, dishonest people."[3] But the trauma of his son's illness brought about a great shift in his thinking, as he witnessed and experienced firsthand the reality of innocent suffering. Concluding that God must be impotent to prevent such agony, he shared the fruit of his theological transformation in his book, *When Bad Things Happen to Good People*, mentioned in the previous chapter. In it he said:

I do not believe the same things about [God] that I did years ago, when I was growing up or when I was a theological student. I recognize His limitations. He is limited in what He can do by laws of nature and by the evolution of human nature and human moral freedom.[4]

The extreme position that God is "limited by laws of nature" depicts Him as an impotent spectator in the tragic unfolding of evil. This was very likely a reaction to the view that many religious people have, and that Rabbi Kushner grew up with—that every catastrophe is the direct expression of the divine. Millions have been turned from God completely because they cherished this misunderstanding. The enemy of God delights in recklessly maiming and destroying whoever he can, then depicting his handiwork as the judgment of God. Though it is erroneous to claim that God *never* acts retributively, it is equally wrong to assume that everything that appears to be divine retribution is. Yet the guilt-ridden human unconscious tends to interpret every misfortune as a heaven-borne "payback" for some sin. From the man who crushes his thumb with a hammer to the hordes of tornado victims, we envision "acts of God" in what are more often the acts of His enemy.

Long before Kushner grappled with the problem of innocent suffering, there was a book written that addressed the issue in the form of a story. The plot is simple. In the mysterious land of Uz a good man lost his children, his fortune and his health in a matter of days. The book travels rapidly through these cataclysmic events and settles itself into a long, tedious dispute between the agonized Job and his four well-meaning but insensitive friends. Three of the friends believe that God is punishing Job for sins of the past, and the fourth thinks that Job's suffering is to prevent him from sinning in the future. Whether corrective or deterrent, all of their theories of suffering have this in common—they interpret his trials as coming directly from God.

The curtain is yanked back even before the show begins, however, when we are told plainly that it is Satan who afflicts Job. The enemy challenged God to allow misery into Job's life, claiming that Job would then curse God to His face.[5]

"Does Job fear God for nothing?" he asked, which translates into, "Job serves you for the perks—protection from harm, riches and honor. Take that away, and he will hate you" (Job 1:9).

In a rare condescension to the devil's terms, God took the challenge and allowed Satan to torment His man. Of course, God knew the character of His friend. He knew that Job would survive the test, because it was the man's habit to depend upon the supporting grace of heaven. Knowing the tensile strength of his servant's faith, God volunteered him for the trial. This means that while Satan was the torturer, God was the One giving permission for the ordeal. God's purpose, obvious from the beginning, was to prove that Job was a "blameless and upright man"—lest the hosts of heaven believe the enemy's accusation that Job was a perks-seeking, time-serving hypocrite (Job 1:8).

But Job and company didn't know all this. All they could see was a man bereaved of his 10 children, sunken in sudden poverty, and covered with hot, oozing boils. The whole picture read divine judgment to the eyes of men who had been schooled to think that God was in the constant business of leveling the scales. And we are much like Job's friends. We have a seemingly innate expectation of justice, fairness, and equity in this earthly life, which leads us to assume that calamities afflict only those who deserve them or somehow need them. Not so, says the book of Job. There is, in this present haphazard realm, such a thing as innocent suffering.

A FOURTH CHOICE—THE GREATER GOOD

"Who sinned, this man or his parents, that he should be born blind?" echoed Jesus' disciples when confronted with inherited blindness. Also believers of the theory of immediate retribution, they tried to trace the curse back to its source.

Jesus' reply was, "Neither ... but it was in order that the works of God might be displayed in him" (John 9:2, 3). "Stop looking for a sin that brought punishment," Jesus was saying. "Rather look for God's overriding purpose in it." Although the doctrine of divine judgment is a true one, we can't expect perfect justice in this sin-ruled world. But we *can* expect God to overrule sin's inequity for His own good and fair purposes. Sin explodes, the shrapnel flies, and God works to bring order and meaning out of chaos. We must look to the future for God's *ruling,* but we can look to the present for Him to *overrule* the sad events of life on planet earth.

Rabbi Kushner understood the random, chaotic character of sin, but he didn't see how that reality could stack up with God's sovereignty. He, like so many of us, expected full justice to come in the here and now. When it obviously didn't, he felt disappointed in his previous conception of God. If God was all-good, he reasoned, He would be *willing* to end suffering. If He was all-powerful, He would be *able* to end suffering. Since the innocent suffer, he thought, God must either want to relieve them, and can't, or be able to relieve them, and won't. C.S. Lewis confirms this apparent dichotomy as the essential "problem of pain" in a book by that name:

> "If God were good, He would wish to make His creatures perfectly happy, and if God were almighty, He would be able to do what He wished. But the creatures are not happy. Therefore God lacks either goodness, or power, or both."[6]

Lewis later points out that while this dilemma seems real to one in the throes of an undeserved misfortune, it is actually a false one. These are not the only three choices. There is a fourth, a biblical perspective—that there is a purpose of greater good behind this present suffering. God *wants* to end suffering, God *wills* to end suffering, but since He is good He allows present suffering for a *greater* good. To His soon-to-be bereaved disciples, Jesus said, "In the world you have tribulation, but take courage; I have overcome the world" (John 16:33). Paul echoed his Master's words as he spoke to his persecuted comrades, "We are afflicted in every way, but not crushed; perplexed, but not despairing; persecuted, but not forsaken; struck down, but not destroyed. … All things are for your sakes, that the grace which is spreading to more and more people may cause the giving of thanks to abound to the glory of God" (2 Corinthians 4:8, 15).

What good could be greater than our pleasure and peace in this earthly life? Simply that we have pleasure and peace in eternity. And that pleasure and peace in eternity is contingent upon the personal and global routing out of the sin that spoiled our pleasure and peace to begin with. If God were to keep us in an eternal state of happiness without dealing with the sin problem, He would ultimately break His own law. This He cannot do. Instead, He must wean us of our attachment to it, that He might finally destroy the sin without destroying the sinner. This weaning He achieves by allowing the chaos of sin to have some access to us. In no other way can its spell be broken.

"Do you want to live with sin?" God asks. "Then let me allow you to see what it is really like behind the gloss. It is a lawless, hideous thing that will rob wide-eyed babies of life and give pleasure and prosperity to the strongest and cruelest. It will weave injustice into the fabric of every society it dominates, exploiting the weak and keeping them in vice and ignorance. It will deceive the masses, then lead them into politically tangled wars where they are harvested for hell by the thousands. It will spread indiscriminate disease that will infect bystanders along with perpetrators. It will keep the struggling masses in poverty, chained to the whims of their gluttonous overlords who feed off their toil and drive them to death without conscience. It will choke the singing birds with the belching of factories that make the rich richer and the poor sick. It will rob the world of a knowledge of the love of God and His care for each creature. It will finally make the soul so dark that it would not enjoy a holy heaven, such that destruction is the only merciful option."

Human hearts don't naturally see sin's trajectory this clearly. Desire determines belief that it is not really so bad. But let the results of it come to our own doorstep, afflicting us or our loved ones, and we are much more likely to see it for what it is. God hopes that this managed, controlled exposure to sin will work like a vaccination, ultimately curing us of its infection. Then He will be able to cleanse the world of sin without destroying sinners. He allows sin to have its power for a period of time, that once every soul has had a chance to see its true nature, He might ultimately take its power. Thus God's acquiescence to sin ultimately results in His triumph over it. If in "mercy" God circumvented the playing out of sin, He would become its great divine "enabler," and thus surrender the rulership of the universe to sin itself.

If the only means whereby we can see sin and Satan for what they are is by viewing their underbelly, and if that underbelly only becomes starkly visible through the lens of suffering, then for God to allow His creatures to suffer is an act of saving mercy, however veiled. Conversely, for God to coddle our sin-enticed selves with uninterrupted pleasure would be to rock us to sleep as the chainsaw murderer was approaching our doorstep. We can see this need for love-driven honesty in the realm of human relationships. C. S. Lewis said:

"It is for people whom we care nothing about that we demand happiness on any terms: with our friends, our lovers, our children, we are exacting and would rather see them suffer much than be happy in contemptible and estranging modes. If God is Love, He is, by definition, something more than mere kindness ... He has paid us the intolerable compliment of loving us, in the deepest, most tragic, most inexorable sense."[7]

But It's All So Unfair!

Oh, but the objection arises, Why do some suffer disproportionately? We don't question God for allowing the smoker to contract cancer nearly so rigorously as we do when an innocent baby is born to sicken and die. Yet that is just the point. How could God acquaint us with the lawless monster if He made it behave within bounds of fairness, only afflicting those who deserved it? A caged gorilla is merely a comical spectacle until it somehow wrenches free of the bars and gains access to those it might maim. How can we come to know the utter cruelty of sin unless it is allowed to run wild? This is just the reason the biblical doctrine of the judgment, far from being a terrorizing embarrassment to Christianity, is a sublime comfort. For it is only when sin is finally dismantled that suffering received will be proportionate to suffering inflicted, the punishment will suit the crime, and the cruel of the earth will be subdued while the innocent are comforted.

The very suffering that Satan uses to turn souls from God is ultimately used by God to turn souls *to* Himself. The starkest example of this divine table-turning is found in the cross. As clear, natural daylight reveals crevices in the skin hidden by artificial indoor lighting, so the light of Calvary revealed the great wrinkle in the face of evil. Jesus said, while standing on the threshold of His death, "Now the ruler of this world shall be cast out" (John 12:31). Jesus did not obfuscate matters with His own selfishness. As He endured the purest form of innocent suffering, the spotless Lamb for sins He did not once commit, the veil on the character of Satan was lifted, revealing him as a deceitful murderer.[8] The unfallen angels, previously bonded to their former comrade, Lucifer, were finally able to detach from him. Since that time lost human souls are cured of their entrancement with the shiny veneer of sin when the light of the cross strips away the cosmetic treatment and reveals its true ugliness. At the cross, Satan himself was deceived into thinking that he could destroy the work of God in the world, even while God used the machinations of hell to establish it.

WHEN GOD SAYS HE DID IT

Now for the rub. A symbol of all innocent suffering, Job's suffering was the doing of Satan. It would be easy for us to gather this fact to ourselves and assume that God had nothing to do with it, and shared no responsibility. This would make the question of innocent suffering easy to solve; Satan is the active bad guy, God is the passive good guy, period. Yet this position would put God in the same unbiblical light that Kushner puts him in. Satan would be, as Peter Stanford, author of *The Devil: A Biography*, said, "the crucial limiting factor on God's omnipotence."[9] Presenting God as the helpless bystander in our conflict with evil flies in the face of the doctrine of divine all-power. Rather, we must recognize that the Bible presents God as the sustainer of all things, including the devil himself, and by extrapolation, sin. No one and nothing, not even the enemy of God and the antithesis of His love, can exist independently of that sustainer. This is why God often speaks in the first person of actively doing something that He merely allows another to do. A case in point is the affliction of Job. Notice the language:

God: "You incited Me against [Job], to ruin him without cause."

Satan: "Put forth Thy hand, now, and touch his bone and his flesh; he will curse Thee to Thy face."

God: "Behold, he is in your power."[10]

First, God lays claim to "ruining" Job by allowing the death of his children and the loss of his fortune. Then Satan taunts God, saying that if He will "put forth [His] hand and touch his bone and flesh"—that is, if God will hurt him physically—Job will surrender his fidelity. Then in an astounding act of seeming cruelty, God consents to the devil's bargain and gives Job into the enemy's power. But notice that He does *not* say, "*I'm* not going to ruin him! *You* do the ruining! *You're* the bad guy!" God will not stoop to play the good cop to Satan's bad cop. To all appearances, God considers His "passive" act of allowing Satan to ruin to be, in some sense, tantamount to Himself doing the ruining. Because of God's omnipotence, and because He is the ongoing sustainer of all living things, He cannot exempt Himself from responsibility for anything that occurs in the universe.

However, notice that the responsibility is an *assumed* one. Since the inception of sin, God has demonstrated His disposition to sacrificially take upon Himself its consequences. As part of that package, He assumed the responsibility for sin's existence. God did not plant the seed of self-exaltation within the angelic Lucifer, but He did allow for the possibility. He did not make Adam's hand pluck the fruit from Eve's hand and chomp down on its flesh, but He did plant the tree in the garden. He gave freedom of choice to His creatures because true love grows in no other soil. Because the growth of this liberty-born love is precious to Him, He embraces as His own the whole mess that this freedom allows. In so doing, He asserts His unvanquished authority in the universe. God will admit of no rival. For Him to fail to take responsibility for sin would be to propose that the hosts of evil are self-sustaining. This is dualism—the belief that both good and evil are powers independent of each other, equal although opposite. Not so, says revelation. Evil exists only by God's permission and power. "I am the Lord, and there is no other, The One forming light and creating darkness, Causing well-being and creating calamity; I am the Lord who does all these" (Isaiah 45:6, 7).

The sovereignty of God accounts perfectly for the times when God speaks of actively doing that which He merely allows another to do, such as Satan's torture of Job. Other examples include:

- The statement that "God hardened Pharaoh's heart" when Pharaoh himself chose to persist in rebellion.[11]
- The statement that God "killed" Saul, Israel's first king, when he actually committed suicide.[12]
- The statement, concerning end-time persecutors who fall under the last great deception, that "God will send upon them a deluding influence so that they might believe what is false."[13]

In these accounts, God seems to puppeteer His created beings, "making" them sin. Yet this assumption does not stack up with the overwhelming evidence that God gives all free choice in matters of sin and salvation.[14] The reason such language is used is because the divine sovereign takes responsibility for what He allows. But responsibility is not blame. Because these events unfolded within God's province, He speaks of Himself as credited for their occurrence, yet it cannot be said that they are God's "fault." These deluded beings made, and will make, their choices, and the blame is theirs.

Someday the enemy of God will bear the blame for the sin he has instigated for more than six millennia. Unfortunately, many will share his fate as they reject the gospel and allow the blame for sin to fall upon them. That we may never find ourselves in that shameful place, God hounds us day and night through His Spirit, leading us to admit our utterly hopeless condition and to fling ourselves upon His mercy. To alarm us into reality, God allows us to taste His wrath against sin in lesser measure than the final, full measure. While Satan delights in making God's children assume that the random afflictions of life are the thunderings of an angry God, he does mimic something real. There are times when God punishes our sins, that we might be led to escape the final condemnation of sin *and* sinners. Both the experiences of life and the biblical record hold much in the way of warnings to the wayward. These are to deter those for whom there is still hope. Although less discernable, these are from love, for as preacher Charles Stanley put it, "Better is the cruelty that hurts and then heals than the kindness that comforts and then kills."

Endnotes

1. Ravi Zacharias, *Jesus Among Other Gods*, (Nashville: Word Publishing Group, 2000), p. 107.

2. The Progeria Research Foundation Webpage, http://www.progeriaresearch. org/whatIs/whatis.htm

3. Harold S. Kushner, *When Bad Things Happen to Good People*, (New York: Schocken Books, 1981), p. 3.

4. *Ibid.*, p. 134.

5. See Job 1:11.

6. C.S. Lewis, *The Problem of Pain*, (New York: Macmillan, 1962), p. 26.

7. *Ibid.*, p. 41.

8. John 8:44.

9. Lewis, p. 113.

10. Selections from Job 2:3–6.

11. The account of the plagues is found in Exodus 7–12. Notice that there are three times when God is said to harden Pharaoh's heart (9:12; 10:20, 27) and at least three times when Pharaoh is said to harden his own heart (8:15, 32; 9:34). The other statements are neutral.

12. 1 Chronicles 10:14.

13. 1 Thessalonians 2:11.

14. Consider 1 Timothy 2:4; 2 Peter 3:9; John 3:16; Revelation 22:17.

Chapter Eight

Thou Hast Destroyed Thyself

K aren Medina started smoking when she was 15 years old. Gradually, "the stealthy puffs in the girls' bathroom became a pack-a-day habit," until, at the age of 44, "Medina began getting what she describes as the worst headaches of her life. A doctor diagnosed migraines. Unconvinced, a pain-stricken Medina drove herself to a hospital emergency room, chain-smoking the entire trip. There, she was given an MRI, a CT scan, and a death sentence: Medina had lung cancer, which had metastasized into multiple tumors in her brain. She was told she had less than a 15 percent chance of still being alive the following" month.

"'Hearing that was a total shock,' admits Medina, who has undergone chemotherapy and radiation treatments. 'Lung cancer happens to everyone but you.'"[1]

The nation's leading killer among cancers, lung cancer exceeds the combined number of deaths from breast, ovarian, and prostate cancers. It claims an estimated 117,000 more lives each year than AIDS. Eighty-six percent of its victims die within five years of diagnosis. Yet it is "as preventable as it is deadly: Nearly 90 percent of lung cancer cases are smoking-related."[2] "'Cigarettes cause lung cancer. It's as simple as that,' [says] Dr. Dan Sullivan, a radiologist for the National Cancer Institute."[3]

WHY SHOULD YOU DIE?

The human body is a wonderfully heroic and resilient organism. Every day, without our giving it a thought, our lungs expand and contract an average of 29,000 times, saturating our blood with life-giving oxygen and ridding it of poisonous carbon dioxide. Our hearts, weighing in at a mere 10 or so ounces, beat more than 100,000 times, pumping an incredible 1,900 gallons of oxygen-enriched blood to every organ and extremity and back again. Our immune systems arrest and summarily execute thousands of inhaled and ingested microscopic invaders, silently saving us from otherwise certain death.[4] Truly, we are "fearfully and wonderfully," even miraculously, made (Psalm 139:14). Yet for all the heroic resilience with which God has imbued our bodies, they have their limits. If we persistently force them to function contrary to nature, depriving them of oxygen and necessary nutrients, overwhelming them with toxins, abusing them in any number of ways, sooner or later something's bound to break. And when it does, if we're honest, we'll be compelled to say with Karen Medina, "I totally blame myself. ... I knew better."[5]

Recognizing our personal responsibility in the matter, we can hardly conclude that lung cancer is a divinely imposed penalty against smokers. Nor can we reasonably assert that cirrhosis of the liver and permanent brain damage are a divine judgment against habitually heavy drinkers, or that sexually transmitted diseases are a divinely imposed penalty against the sexually promiscuous. On the contrary, all of these outcomes eloquently testify to the innate destructiveness of sin, as that which we have worked into our minds and bodies visibly and palpably works itself back out.

This is the primary sense in which God says that those who make destructive choices destroy *themselves* (See Hosea 13:9 KJV). Correctly discerning the source of our trouble, He puts His finger on the plague spot. If we "sow the wind" we will surely "reap the whirlwind," as the causes we set into motion bring about their logical and inevitable effects (Hosea 8:7). Even so, He doesn't despise us for our perversity. He feels our collective pain as if it were His own, as we groan under our crushing burden, "Our offenses and sins weigh us down, and we are wasting away because of them. How then can we live?" (Ezekiel 33:10 NIV). With divine empathy, He responds, "As I live … I have no pleasure in the death of the wicked, but that the wicked turn from his way and live. Turn, turn from your evil ways! For why should you die?" (Ezekiel 33:11).

In Him All Things Consist

Still, we can't exactly say that God has no part in the matter. As we discussed in our last chapter, though He is not responsible for our choices, neither is He divorced from their outcomes. As the Creator and sustainer of life and the laws that govern it, He is intimately involved in every facet of the human experience. "For by him all things were created: things in heaven and on earth, visible and invisible. … And in him all things hold together" (Colossians 1:16, 17 NIV). This means that God didn't merely establish creation according to certain laws, wind up the mechanism, and stand back to watch it run down, as deism asserts. Rather, life and the laws that govern it flow continually from His very being, as He personally, proactively "uphold[s] all things by the word of His power" (Hebrews 1:3). His laws of life are themselves living laws, perpetually proceeding from and establishing the substance of His inmost thoughts.

And so we find ourselves caught in the crossfire between our death-dealing sin and God's life-giving law. When we sin by violating the laws of our very beings, we hurt ourselves, because sin is innately destructive. And because it is innately destructive, it is diametrically opposed to divinely established and sustained laws of life, which are, by definition, diametrically opposed to our sin. Sin is anti-life, and God's natural laws are anti-sin. There can be no agreement between them. Yet even while they repel each other in principle, they seize upon each other in effect, careening out their irreconcilable enmity in a cataclysmic dance to the death. Sin destroys us, and God's law destroys sin, which inhabits us.

Paul describes this antagonistic relationship between divine law and sin like this:

> "The commandment, which was to bring life, I found to bring death. For sin, taking occasion by the commandment, deceived me, and by it killed me. Therefore the law is holy, and the commandment holy and just and good. ... But sin, that it might appear sin, was producing death in me through what is good, so that sin through the commandment might become exceedingly sinful" (Romans 7:10–13).

In short, while the concrete consequences of our life-destroying choices can't be said to constitute a divine judgment against *us*, they do speak of a divine judgment against our *sin*. God says such naturalistic "judgment springs up like hemlock in the furrows of the field," revealing His disapproval of, and inability to bless, our harmful choices even as we reap their poisonous harvest (Hosea 10:4). Extended in mercy to the sinner, such judgment against sin warns us to separate ourselves from its baleful influence before it's too late—before we are completely ruined by it. It alerts us to our danger, as pain alerts to disease and injury and provides us with the motivation to respond constructively. Yet as inevitable and universally operative as such naturalistic intrinsic justice is, it can never be the complete revelation of cosmic justice that some have styled it. While it is specific as to sin, it is not sufficiently specific to the sinner, as the innocent suffer with the guilty due to sin's corporate, chaotic nature. As has been said, sin explodes, the shrapnel flies, and we are appalled at its indiscriminate fallout.

As the smoking, pregnant mother inhales more than 4,000 chemicals, including 43 known carcinogens, with each cigarette,[6] her unborn child absorbs those same chemicals and carcinogens through the maternal blood supply, vastly increasing its susceptibility to disease and death via low birth weight, preterm birth, spontaneous abortion, and sudden infant death syndrome.[7] As the alcoholic causes irreversible damage to his heart, liver, kidneys, stomach, brain and nervous system, he also positions himself to become a contributing cause of the nation's annual 513,000 alcohol-related traffic injuries and 17,000 fatalities.[8] And what about the HIV-positive person who callously transmits his deadly disease to his uninformed spouse, who then transmits it to the child of their union?[9]

While intrinsic justice is continually at work, exerting itself through the bodies and minds of responsible parties, its indiscriminate impact on innocent bystanders renders it an imperfect revelation of divine justice. Yet as obscured as it is by the corporate, chaotic fallout of sin, it constitutes the starting point of the justice continuum, implying and prefiguring a more explicitly moral and individualized dimension to justice.

BE HOLY, BECAUSE I AM HOLY

"For since the creation of the world [God's] invisible attributes are clearly seen, being understood by the things that are made, even His eternal power and Godhead, so that [those who suppress the truth] are without excuse" (Romans 1:20). Just as a visible creation implies the existence and agency of an invisible, authoritative Creator, so natural laws imply the existence and operation of underlying, authoritative moral and spiritual laws. As C.S. Lewis put it in his book, *Mere Christianity*:

> "Each man is at every moment subjected to several different sets of law but there is only one of these which he is free to disobey. As a body, he is subjected to gravitation and cannot disobey it. ... As an organism, he is subjected to various biological laws which he cannot disobey any more than an animal can. That is, he cannot disobey those laws which he shares with other things; but the law which is peculiar to his human nature, the law he does not share with animals or vegetables or inorganic things, is the one he can disobey if he chooses."[10]

This law that is peculiar to human beings, which requires but cannot compel our obedience, makes explicit what is implicit in natural law—that the seeds of our choices not only bring a harvest after their own kind, they are also something for which we, as moral beings, are held morally responsible. For, unlike any other creature, humans are created in the "image of God" (Genesis 1:27; 9:6). This includes a *moral* likeness to Him, with all that implies—the capacity for moral perception, reflection, and decision, with its attendant accountability (See Colossians 3:10; James 3:9).

Far from being arbitrary and divorced from reality, the universal moral law to which humanity is accountable derives from the living and authoritative character of the Creator Himself. As Christian ethicist Norman Geisler has said:

"The ethical imperatives that God gives are in accord
with his unchangeable moral character. That is, God
wills what is right in accordance with his own moral
attributes. 'Be holy, because I am holy,' the Lord
commanded Israel (Leviticus 11:45). 'Be perfect,
therefore, as your heavenly Father is perfect,' Jesus
said to his disciples (Matthew 5:48). 'It is impossible
for God to lie' (Hebrews 6:18). So we should not lie
either. 'God is love' (1 John 4:16), and so Jesus said,
'Love your neighbor as yourself' (Matthew 22:39)."[11]

God demonstrated this equivalency between His
unchanging moral character and these ethical imperatives
by distilling them into 10 comprehensive precepts and
engraving them into tables of stone with His own hand (See
Exodus 32:16; Deuteronomy 10:4). From Mount Sinai, He
spoke these 10 timeless, universal precepts of righteousness
for the benefit of humanity: [12]

1. There is but one God; worship Him only.
2. Do not worship the works of your own hands.
3. Do not take God's name in vain.
4. Keep the seventh day holy, by resting from your
   works.
5. Honor your parents.
6. Do not commit murder.
7. Do not commit adultery.
8. Do not steal.
9. Do not bear false witness.
10. Do not desire what belongs to others.

These 10 comprehensive precepts of life were, in turn,
practically and succinctly summarized by Jesus, as He
echoed the words He originally spoke to the Israelites in
the wilderness:

> "'Love the Lord your God with all your heart and
> with all your soul and with all your mind.' This
> is the first and greatest commandment. And the
> second is like it: 'Love your neighbor as yourself.'
> All the Law and the Prophets hang on these two
> commandments" (Matthew 22:37–40 NIV).[13]

Before the Fall, such pure, principled, self-forgetful love
had been innate to humanity, as our hearts and minds moved
in moral synchronism with God's. But with the entrance of
sin, we expelled God's indwelling character, and that which
had been intrinsic to humanity became extrinsic. The great
moral law of love and life, which was once descriptive of
our inmost beings, became *prescriptive*—it no longer spoke
of who we *were*, but of who we *ought to be*. Humanity has
ever since found itself perched on the points of a dilemma
consisting of these two prongs:

"First, that human beings, all over the earth, have this
curious idea that they *ought* to behave in a certain way, and
cannot really get rid of it. Secondly, that they *do not* in fact
behave in that way. They know the Law of [Human] Nature;
they break it. These two facts are the foundation of all clear
thinking about ourselves and the universe we live in."[14]

You *Can* Go Home Again

These are the facts of our condition. There is only one
law of life in the universe, and this law we are naturally
disinclined and unable to obey. This law informs us that we
are not only people who tend to make choices that bring life-
destroying consequences, but we are also people who have so
placed ourselves out of harmony with its just and necessary
ethical imperatives that we have rendered ourselves unsafe
and unworthy to be entrusted with the gift of eternal life.
This is our legacy in Adam. Though we did not personally

participate in his original sin, and have "not sinned according to the likeness of [his] transgression," we have inherited his rebellious nature (Romans 5:14). With him, we have been understandably excluded from paradise, and of ourselves we can't go home again.

Yet there is One who is able to take us back; one person who is worthy to be entrusted with the gift of life, and who has been given "authority over all flesh, that He should give eternal life to as many as [God has] given Him" (John 17:2): "Worthy is *the Lamb* who was slain To receive power and riches and wisdom, And strength and honor and glory and blessing!" (Revelation 5:12, emphasis supplied). He is worthy because He *was slain.* Every day of His life, Jesus offered up self to be slain on the cross of self-denial; in the end, He surrendered Himself up to be slain utterly by our sin and its just judgment, becoming "obedient to the point of death, even the death of the cross" (Philippians 2:8). In His life and His death, Jesus exemplified and established the law of life in human flesh. When we enshrine Him in our hearts, we enshrine the living law of life.

This is what God means when He says,

"I will put My law in their minds, and write it on their hearts" (Jeremiah 31:33).

"I will give you a new heart and put a new spirit within you; I will take the heart of stone out of your flesh and give you a heart of flesh. I will put My Spirit within you and cause you to walk in My statutes, and you will keep My judgments and do them. ... you shall be My people, and I will be your God" (Ezekiel 36:26–28).

This is the way back to paradise, the one and only way of life. It is the first, last and best that God has to offer us—Himself, in the person of the Son. He has nothing greater or more effectual to give. If we willfully, persistently "neglect so great a salvation," what is left to us "but a certain fearful expectation of judgment, and fiery indignation" (Hebrews 2:3; 10:27)? To intelligently and purposefully reject the only way of life is to sever ourselves from its transforming power and set ourselves up as incorrigible enemies of the only good and just government in the universe.

THERE IS NO SAVIOR BESIDES ME

This is the second sense in which God says to the spiritually resistant, "Thou hast destroyed thyself" (Hosea 13:9, KJV). They leave Him no recourse but to relate to them judgmentally—first correctively, according to His discretion, and finally, punitively. The deeper they plunge into sin, the more they become a danger to themselves and others, the greater their moral accountability. At the same time, the more inextricably entwined with sin they become. To paraphrase Hosea 9:10, "When they separate themselves to shame, they become an abomination like the thing they love." To separate oneself to sin is to become its moral equivalent and suffer its eternal fate.

Yet such is the hopeful persistence of redeeming love that, even as God confronts hardened rebels with the scathing truth, "Thou hast destroyed thyself," He pleads, "but in me is thine help. I will be thy king: where is any other that may save thee in all thy cities? ... There is no savior besides Me" (Hosea 13:9, 10 KJV; v. 4 NKJV). For those who listen and believe, there is deliverance and transformation. For those who persistently refuse, there must be a ratcheting up of intensity on the judgment continuum, as justice proceeds from intrinsic consequences to increasingly extrinsic interventions.

Endnotes

1. Ellie McGrath, "What You Don't Know about Women and Lung Cancer," http://www.4woman.gov/editor/Apr01/Apr01.htm

2. *Ibid.*

3. Troy Goodman, "Lung Cancer Ranks Among Deadliest, Most Neglected Cancers," http://www.cnn.com/2000/HEALTH/cancer/11/16/lung.cancer/index.html

4. Research done through www.howstuffworks.com

5. McGrath.

6. See "What's Really in Cigarettes?" http://www.carlmont.seq.org/students/cigarettes.html

7. See "Effect of maternal cigarette smoking on pregnancy complications and sudden infant death syndrome," J.R. DiFranza and R.A. Lew, National Library of Medicine, http://www.ncbi.nlm.nih.gov/entrez/query.fcgi?cmd =Retrieve&db=PubMed&list_uids=7699353&dopt=Abstract; "Effects of Maternal Cigarette Smoking on Birth Weight and Preterm Birth—Ohio, 1989," *Morbidity and Mortality Weekly Report*, Centers for Disease Control, http://www.cdc.gov/epo/mmwr/preview/mmwrhtml/00001782.htm

8. Information obtained through the National Institute on Alcohol Abuse and Alcoholism: www.niaaa.nih.gov/; Mothers Against Drunk Driving: www.madd.org

9. Something that happens in third-world countries, and India, with terrifying frequency. See "AIDS and marriage: A double ostracism," http://www.rediff.com/news/1999/nov/30hiv.htm

10. C.S. Lewis, *Mere Christianity,* revised and amplified edition (San Francisco: HarperCollins, 2001), pp. 4, 5.

11. Norman Geisler, *Christian Ethics* (Grand Rapids, MI: Baker Book House, 1989), p. 22.

12. Paraphrase of Exodus 20:1–17.

13. See Deuteronomy 6:5; Leviticus 19:18.

14. Lewis, p. 8, emphasis supplied.

Chapter Nine

How Can I Give You Up?

Eighteenth century revivalist Jonathan Edwards knew how to keep a congregation on the edge of its seat. In fact, record has it that one of his sermons, "Sinners in the Hands of an Angry God," literally "caused his congregation to rise weeping and moaning from their seats," while "some of the converted were so obsessed by his fiery descriptions of eternal damnation that they contemplated suicide."[1] With such fearsome word pictures as these did Edwards unsettle his listeners:

> "The God that holds you over the pit of hell, much as one holds a spider, or some loathsome insect over the fire, abhors you, and is dreadfully provoked: His wrath towards you burns like fire; He looks upon you as worthy of nothing else, but to be cast into the fire; He is of purer eyes than to bear to have you in His sight; you are ten thousand times more abominable in His eyes than the most hateful venomous serpent is in ours."[2]

Yet such word pictures are not only unsettling and repugnant, they are also rankly unbiblical. God has never represented Himself as hating, or desiring the destruction of, the unconverted. Though He must deal with the sin problem for the good of His universe, His posture toward His unbelieving children is not that of an angry adversary,[3] but of a longsuffering advocate. If we find this hard to believe, all we need to do is look at Jesus.

When Philip, struggling to conceptualize the God he thought he'd never seen, pleaded, " 'Lord, show us the Father, and it is sufficient for us,' Jesus assured him, 'He who has seen Me has seen the Father' " (John 14:8, 9). If we want to "see" God's attitude toward lost humanity, we must look at Jesus. Even more to the point in our study of justice, if we want to see a graphic portrayal of how God "gives up" the incorrigibly rebellious to intrinsic and extrinsic judgment, we can look at Jesus' magnanimous treatment of His betrayer.

One of You Is a Devil

Judas Iscariot was an artful, ambitious Judean[4] who joined himself to Jesus' ragtag band of Galilean followers as the promising young teacher was gaining in popularity. A self-styled aristocrat in the midst of an otherwise dirty dozen comprised of rough-hewn fishermen, reformed tax collectors and political zealots, Judas eschewed their clumsy attempts at social climbing[5] in favor of his own more subtle efforts at upward mobility. Having established himself as the group's treasurer, entrusted with purchasing supplies and doling out alms for the poor, he compensated himself for his trouble by periodically appropriating a "paycheck" from their meager funds (See John 12:6; 13:29). After all, he reasoned, the up-and-coming prime minister of Jesus' soon-to-be-established kingdom was entitled to a few perks. Who could fault him for making sure he got what was coming to him?

As seriously flawed as he was, Jesus saw in him, as He sees in every flawed soul, someone who could respond to

His love. Knowing he was a thief, Jesus continued to entrust him with the struggling little band's paltry income, giving him opportunity to reflect and repent. Investing him with power to heal the sick and cast out demons, Jesus included him among the 70 evangelists in the infant church's first, and spectacularly successful, large-scale outreach (See Luke 10:1–17; Mark 6:7–13). Patiently He worked around the sensitive ego, tenderly He massaged the hard heart, until as much transforming love was lavished on Judas as on any of the disciples.

Yet after two years of soaking up Jesus' unremitting attention, Judas had so permitted Satan to imbue him with his own attributes that Jesus acknowledged, "Have I not chosen you, the Twelve? Yet one of you is a devil!" (John 6:70 NIV). Still, He didn't openly rebuke His proud disciple for another year, when Judas stepped over the line by publicly humiliating Mary Magdalene for pouring out her heart and all her substance on Jesus as she anointed Him for His burial (See John 12:1–8; Matthew 26:12). Smarting under that deserved correction, and convinced that Jesus would never be the sort of Messiah he had envisioned, Judas stalked off "to the chief priests to betray Him to them" for "thirty pieces of silver"—the price of a slave (Mark 14:10; Matthew 26:15). Pride, greed and ambition had been secretly indulged until they eventually won out over integrity, self-respect and loyalty to his best friend.

Yet such is the self-effacing love of Christ that He reached out to Judas even on the night of his betrayal. Tenderly, He washed the feet of His false friend, His forgiving eyes penetrating deeply into Judas' guilty ones, until Judas was convinced that Jesus read his treacherous heart and loved him in spite of it. In those last critical moments of Judas' probation, as his fading inclination toward repentance hung so tenuously in the balance, agonized agape did all that was in its power to win his disaffected heart. In the words of an insightful writer:

"Jesus hungered for [Judas'] soul. He felt for him such a burden as for Jerusalem when He wept over the doomed city. His heart was crying, *How can I give thee up?* The constraining power of that love was felt by Judas. When the Saviour's hands were bathing those soiled feet, and wiping them with the towel, the heart of Judas thrilled through and through with the impulse then and there to confess his sin. But he would not humble himself. He hardened his heart against repentance; and the old impulses, for the moment put aside, again controlled him."[6]

Jesus had no choice but to reluctantly permit what He would not prevent. As "Satan entered" His lost disciple, Jesus urged, "What you do, do quickly" (John 13:27). Having set his face like a flint against the only One who stood between him and the powers of darkness, Judas "went out immediately. And it was night"—eternal night—for his soul (v. 30).

WOE TO THEM WHEN I DEPART FROM THEM!

It's a fearful thing to be given up by the living God. It's a fearful thing to remove ourselves from the protection of the only One who can save us from ourselves and our "adversary the devil," who "walks about like a roaring lion, seeking whom he may devour" (1 Peter 5:8). It's a fearful thing to render ourselves liable to judgment. Under such circumstances it would be better for us, as Jesus said of Judas, if we had never been born.[7] Knowing the horror that must follow divine abandonment, God says of the spiritually incorrigible, "Woe to them when I depart from them!" (Hosea 9:12).

To spare us from that horror, God spells out some of what it entails in Romans 1 and 2. He begins by explaining, through the apostle Paul, what it is that arouses His righteous anger: "For the wrath of God is revealed from heaven against all *ungodliness and unrighteousness* of men, who suppress the truth in unrighteousness" (Romans 1:18, emphasis supplied). It can never be overemphasized that God's wrath is not primarily against *sinners*, but against *sin*—against ungodliness and unrighteousness. First, against ungodliness, which is the inner attitude of rebellion, the fountainhead of corruption, then against unrighteousness, which is its outflow in the form of acts of immorality and injustice.

The implications of this are astounding. This means that when God looks at our world and sees that "there is none who does good, no, not one," that we have "together become unprofitable," He nevertheless differentiates, as long as possible, between us and our indwelling sin (Romans 3:12). Exercising faith in what we might become in Christ, God envisions us separated from our ungodliness and unrighteousness, and does everything in His power to bring this about. But if we persistently resist His efforts to disentangle us from sin, He must reach the point when He can no longer honestly differentiate us from it. He must withdraw His rejected Holy Spirit and say of us, as He said of ancient Israel, "Ephraim is joined to idols, Let him alone" (Hosea 4:17). He must give us up to the intrinsic and extrinsic consequences of our choices.

Comprehended in sin's intrinsic consequences are a host of degenerative spiritual, psychological, social, and physical processes. These include the degradation and destruction of our characters, our health and our relationships, vulnerability to demonic oppression and possession, and unprotected exposure to the ravages of a hostile social and natural environment. Romans 1:18–32 focuses on the intrinsic consequences experienced by those "who suppress the truth in unrighteousness" and "receiv[e] *in themselves* the penalty of their error which [is] due" (Romans 1:18, 27).

- They lose the ability to comprehend or care about spiritual things, becoming "futile in their thoughts" and "darkened" in "their foolish hearts" (v. 21).
- They become enslaved to "uncleanness in the lusts of their hearts, to dishonor their bodies among themselves" (v. 24).
- They become controlled by their "vile passions" (v. 26).
- They develop "a debased mind, to do those things which are not fitting"—"things" that include the entire spectrum of sins to which the human race is subject: "sexual immorality, ... covetousness, maliciousness; ... envy, murder, strife, deceit, evil-mindedness"—in short, "all unrighteousness" (vs. 28, 29).

In whatever way it manifests itself, such a self-caused moral meltdown equates to moral suicide. The story of King Saul provides a cautionary tale of how one who has committed such moral suicide can slip into a spiral of self-destruction that ultimately ends in literal suicide.[8]

At first humbled by his divine appointment as Israel's first king, Saul subsequently succumbed to the intoxication of power and popularity. Attributing his success to innate goodness and giftedness, he nurtured his ego and hardened his heart until he became insensible to the pleadings of the Holy Spirit. No longer "little in [his] own eyes," he bullied his sons, tyrannized his subjects, blatantly disregarded divine directives, and blamed everyone else for his moral failures (1 Samuel 15:17). His conscience seared, his will irreversibly bent toward rebellion, his ambitions and affections decisively pitted against his Maker, he left God with no choice but to give him up to the harrowing consequences of his choices and abandon him as king.

Bereft of a moral compass, literally and figuratively haunted by the demons of depression and despair, Saul became a pawn of the devil, who drew him into an ever more convoluted web of intrigue and paranoia. Having rendered himself incapable of receiving comfort and guidance from the God he had rejected, Saul, in a moment of crisis, sought solace from a witch (1 Samuel 28). Fully and finally ensnared by Satan, he was dead within 24 hours, slain by his own hand.

Nor is such existential tragedy solely the domain of ancient biblical history. We see it repeated over and over again in the lives of contemporary cultural icons. We hear its nihilistic echoes in writings such as the recently released *Journals*, rock legend Kurt Cobain's posthumously published diaries. Tormented by his self-destructive impulses and burdened by too much success too soon, Cobain spiraled into a heroin addiction cycle in which he seesawed between using and kicking. During his first agonizing rehabilitation, Cobain lamented, "Drug withdrawal is everything you've ever heard. You puke, you [flail] around, you sweat. ... It's evil. Leave it alone." Two heroin-haunted years later, Cobain shot himself in his Seattle, Washington, home, leaving behind a suicide note that read, in part, "I don't know where I'm going. I just can't be here anymore."[9]

Such intrinsic torment might seem hell enough to pay for a self-initiated god-forsaken life. Yet while such torment is certainly hell on earth for those who experience it, not all who decisively turn their backs on God endure such a dramatic and excruciating unraveling. Some morally insensate souls seem hardly to suffer a pang of conscience for the evil they foist on their fellow beings. Yet regardless of how sensible the lost may or may not be to their damaged and damaging condition, they must still answer to the moral and judicial implications of their choices. They must account for their actions and their influence. So God must also give up the incorrigible to the extrinsic consequences of their sin, sometimes in this life,[10] always in the judgment to come. As our Romans passage makes explicit:

"In accordance with your hardness and your impenitent heart you are treasuring up for yourself wrath in the day of wrath and revelation of the righteous judgment of God who 'will render to each one according to his deeds': eternal life to those who by patient continuance in doing good seek for glory, honor, and immortality; but to those who are self-seeking and do not obey the truth, but obey unrighteousness—indignation and wrath, tribulation and anguish, on every soul of man who does evil. ... For there is no partiality with God" (Romans 2:5–9, 11).

Indeed, as Jesus said of Judas, it would be better not to have been born than to find ourselves unnecessarily facing a life's record of unbelief, ungodliness and unrighteousness—not because God is cruelly unjust, but because He is infinitely just.

How Does He Give Them Up?

How, then, does God give up people to extrinsic judgment in this life? How does He both "passively" abandon and "actively" execute judgment upon them?

David said of God, "Where can I go from Your Spirit? Or where can I flee from Your presence? If I ascend into heaven, You are there; If I make my bed in hell, behold, You are there" (Psalms 139:7, 8). As long as life shall last, it is not possible for human beings to ever truly absent themselves from the presence of God. Though His Holy Spirit must cease pleading with the consciences of those who turn a deaf ear, His life-giving Spirit continues to sustain them; whatever they experience, it is because He enables them. For that reason, when God gives people up to judgment, there is a sense in which He hands them over from one part of

Himself to another—from the "Advocate" to the "Judge of all the earth" (See 1 John 2:1; Genesis 18:25).

When the Lord lamented of His rebellious people, "How can I *give you up*, Ephraim? How can I *hand you over*, Israel?" He added, "How can I *make you* like Admah? How can I *set you* like Zeboiim? My heart churns within Me; My sympathy is stirred" (Hosea 11:8, emphasis supplied). What was it that happened to Admah and Zeboiim, and who was it that brought it about?

"The whole land is brimstone, salt, and burning; it is not sown, nor does it bear, nor does any grass grow there, like the overthrow of Sodom and Gomorrah, *Admah and Zeboiim, which the Lord overthrew in His anger and His wrath*" (Deuteronomy 29:23, emphasis supplied).

God Himself rained fire and brimstone on Admah and Zeboiim, Sodom and Gomorrah. He is the One who executed the judgment to which He had given them up. And so His heart churns within Him as He deliberates as to when this crucial transfer must take place, when He must "hand us over" from the advocate to the prosecutor. On what basis, then, does God decide when individuals and corporate entities must be handed over to judgment? What is the biblical criterion?

I Am, and There Is No One Else Besides Me

Isaiah 47 provides a fascinating glimpse into the psycho-spiritual dynamics of an individual or corporate entity that has become ripe for judgment. Prophesying of the retribution that would be executed upon Babylon approximately 200 years before it happened, Isaiah notes the arrogance and delusion that defined that nation's self-perception:

"Therefore hear this now, you who are given to pleasures, Who dwell securely, Who say in your heart, 'I am, and there is no one else besides me; I shall not sit as a widow, Nor shall I know the loss of children.' ... For you have trusted in your wickedness; you have said, 'No one sees me;' your wisdom and your knowledge have warped you" (Isaiah 47:8, 10).

Babylon's "warped" self-perception was characterized by four distinctive, related and willful delusions:

I am. Presumptuously claiming self-existence, Babylon echoed God's singular description of Himself to Moses, "I AM WHO I AM. ... Thus you shall say to the children of Israel, 'I AM has sent me to you' " (Exodus 3:14).

There is no one else besides me. Snugly wrapped in its delusion of self-existence, Babylon gave itself up to rampant narcissism; perceiving itself as preeminent, it submitted itself to no higher law than its own desires.

No one sees me. Having become its own god and a world unto itself, Babylon perceived itself to be morally impenetrable and unaccountable—i.e., "If there is no God to see my sin, it didn't happen."

I shall not sit as a widow, neither shall I know the loss of children. Secure in its delusion of moral unaccountability, Babylon naturally concluded that it was exempt from penalty and loss.

Such an arrogant, delusive self-perception equates with what psychiatrist M. Scott Peck describes as "malignant narcissism":

"Malignant narcissism is characterized by an unsubmitted will. All adults who are mentally healthy submit themselves one way or another to something higher than themselves, be it God or truth or love or some other ideal. They do what God wants them to do rather than what they would desire. 'Thy will, not mine, be done,' the God-submitted person says. They believe in what is true rather than what they would like to be true. ... To a greater or lesser degree, all mentally healthy individuals submit themselves to the demands of their own conscience. Not so the evil, however. In the conflict between their guilt and their will, it is the guilt that must go and the will that must win." [11]

Paul describes such a relentlessly willful, morally unsubmitted person as "having their conscience seared with a hot iron" (1 Timothy 4:2, KJV). Such conscienceless, "malignant narcissism" can't be kept to itself. As C.S. Lewis has noted, "Every vice leads to cruelty." [12] Given time, ungodliness invariably translates into oppressive behavior that rightly ignites God's protective wrath in behalf of the oppressed. Repeatedly—whether it is Judas or Saul or arrogant, luxurious Babylon—God tells us that when people and nations build themselves up at the expense of others, when they habitually subjugate justice to the corrupt demands of self-interest, they become slated for extrinsic judgment:

"Woe to those who decree unrighteous decrees, Who write misfortune, Which they have prescribed To rob the needy of justice, And to take what is right from the poor of My people, That widows may be their prey, And that they may rob the fatherless" (Isaiah 10:1, 2).

"Therefore, because you tread down the poor And take grain taxes from him, Though you have built houses of hewn stone, Yet you shall not dwell in them; You have planted pleasant vineyards, But you shall not drink wine from them. For I know your manifold transgressions And your mighty sins. You afflict the just and take bribes; You divert the poor from justice at the gate" (Amos 5:11, 12).

This refrain is repeated again and again throughout the Bible. When individuals and corporate entities spiral into irreversible spiritual and moral decline, giving themselves over to "manifold transgressions and ... mighty sins," advantaging themselves by defrauding those whom they should be helping with their resources, they have overstepped their boundaries. God alone knows when that line of demarcation has been crossed. And when it has, the divine equalizer steps in, according to His discretion, to set things right.

Endnotes

1. "Edwards, Jonathan," Microsoft Encarta Online Encyclopedia 2003, s.v. "Edwards, Jonathan," http://encarta.msn.com copyright 1997–2003 Microsoft Corporation. All Rights Reserved.

2. Jonathan Edwards, "Sinners in the Hands of an Angry God," taken from www.ccel.org/e/edwards/sermons/sinners.html

3. This is, in fact, the posture of Satan, whose name means "adversary" or "hater." This hostile posture toward humanity he continually attempts to attach to God; history testifies to the phenomenal success of his strategy.

4. Iscariot, from the Greek *Iskarioth*, is usually considered to be derived from the Hebrew *ish Queriyoth*, "man of Kerioth," a town in the southernmost part of Judah, near Hebron.

5. See Matthew 20:20–24; Mark 10:35–41.

6. Ellen G. White, *The Desire of Ages* (Mountain View, CA: Pacific Press Publishing Association, 1940), p. 645, emphasis supplied.

7. See Matthew 26:24; Mark 14:21; Luke 22:22.

8. See 1 Samuel 9–31 for the saga of Saul.

9. Excerpted from Lorraine Ali, "Cries From the Heart," *Newsweek*, October 28, 2002.

10. While it's true that God also executes disciplinary judgments against the still salvageable, (those "whom the Lord loves He chastens," Hebrews 12:6), when the Bible speaks of His "giving up" sinners to the intrinsic and extrinsic consequences of their choices, the indication is that He has done all He can to save them and there is nothing left but retributive judgment.

11. M. Scott Peck, MD, *People of the Lie* (New York: A Touchstone Book, published by Simon & Schuster, 1983), p. 78.

12. C.S. Lewis, *The Problem of Pain* (New York: HarperCollins Publishers, Inc., 1996), p. 59.

Chapter Ten

When God Stops Winking

"I climbed Hikiyama Hill and looked down. I saw that Hiroshima had disappeared. I was shocked by the sight. ... Of course I saw many dreadful scenes after that—but that experience, looking down and finding nothing left of Hiroshima—was so shocking that I simply can't express what I felt. ... Hiroshima didn't exist—that was mainly what I saw—Hiroshima just didn't exist."
—Richard Rhodes, *The Making of the Atomic Bomb* [1]

When Keiko Sasaki saw his grandmother coming home after a week-long trip to Hiroshima, he asked, "Where's mother?" Keiko's grandma had heard of the bomb, and had gone to find her daughter who lived there.

"I brought her on my back," his grandmother said.

Keiko relates what happened next:

"I was happy and shouted 'Mummy!' But when I looked closely, I saw she was only carrying a rucksack. I was disappointed. ... Then my grandmother put the rucksack down and took some bones out of it and showed them to everybody. There were my mother's gold tooth and a piece of her elbow bone. I still didn't understand." [2]

113

How could he understand? How could he know, at a mere six years old, that in the wee hours of August 6, 1945, the B-29 bomber Enola Gay, carrying a single four-ton, uranium-cored atomic device dubbed "Little Boy," was dropped on Hiroshima, detonating about 2,000 feet above the ground? How could a child conceive that the blast demolished three-fifths of the city within seconds? How could he comprehend that three days later a similar bomb, "Fat Man," was dropped on Nagasaki? And that a day later the Japanese government offered to surrender? How could he comprehend the world's first and only full encounter with atomic warfare, which took its toll of well over 100,000 people? How *could* Keiko understand, when even the reality of his mother's death escaped him?

It's hard to stomach stories of mass carnage. We are designed with empathic powers that, unless they are blunted to death, cause us to feel something of others' pain. More than this, sensitive human beings recoil from committing acts of violence. Made in God's image, we have a seemingly natural immunity to inflicting death upon our fellow man. According to military psychologist David Grossman, "Every species, with a few exceptions, has a hardwired resistance to killing its own kind." Grossman coined the term "killology" to refer to the process of training soldiers to bypass this natural hesitancy. He later reported the success of this process:

> "During the Civil War, the firing rate was as low as 15 percent. … A 15 percent firing rate among riflemen is like a 15 percent literacy rate among librarians. … By the Korean War, around 55 percent of the soldiers were willing to fire to kill. And by Vietnam, the rate rose to over 90 percent."[3]

If human beings have an internal resistance to violence, how much more the God in whose image we are made? Any humane qualities we possess are inspired by the Spirit of

God—how much more does God Himself recoil from the task of destruction? Yet He who is the giver of life has at times taken life. In fact, a surface reading of some of the divine judgments of biblical history remind us of the episodes of mass destruction that have marked recent human history. In the fire and brimstone that showered Sodom and Gomorrah we see a strange resemblance to the atomic brimstone of Hiroshima and Nagasaki. While it is true that God has the *right* to destroy those He has created, this answer alone does not satisfy the sensitive heart's quest to understand how a loving God can punish and destroy. We must probe more deeply.

JEWISH THUNDER, CHRISTIAN SUNBEAMS?

Often the Old Testament is cited as the home of the angry, wrath-mongering tyrant, and the New Testament the abode of the peace-loving, placid Messiah. Jewish lightning and thunder are contrasted with Christian sunbeams. This is an unfair and biased view, based upon a surface perusal of both testaments. Biblically, Jesus is identified as the judge and lawgiver, and the divine disciplinarian of Israel.[4] In truth, the New Testament exhibits no shame toward the Old Testament judgments, but rather uses them as illustrations of judgment to come. The most direct and forceful of the early judgments are unabashedly said to be prophetic pictures of the final punishment of the wicked. The fires of Sodom are said to be "exhibited as an example, in undergoing the punishment of eternal fire" (Jude 7).[5] If wrath is an indication of cruelty, God hasn't gotten any nicer since Sodom and Gomorrah. Fortunately, wrath is not an indication of cruelty. It is, like all the expressions of God, a demonstration of pure, selfless love. An examination of the earliest, most extrinsic of divine judgments will bear this out.

Let us scroll back to a point previous to our existence as a race. Heaven is in turmoil. Lucifer's revolution has yielded him a mass of angelic devotees. After a spiritual struggle of unknown length, Lucifer and his angels are "thrown down to the earth" (Revelation 12:9). This banishment from the courts of heaven marks the end of their opportunity for repentance. There is no turning back for these god-forsaken goblins, for they have resisted heaven's pleading voice until it can no longer be heard. The original Hell's Angels are now "reserved for judgment" and a destructive fire is planned for them and their leader (2 Peter 2:4).[6]

In this alpha of judgments, the first time God ever lifted a finger in such retribution, we see a principle that runs like a thread throughout the story of redemption. God reserves His most forceful, direct dealings with sin—His extrinsic judgments—for times when the soul is utterly hardened and hopeless. This "malignant narcissism" had rotted the soul of Lucifer and his followers until they had sealed their wills against the God of heaven. Tragically, humans have at times emulated the fallen angels and have brought a similar fate upon themselves.

THE FLOOD

Scroll forward to life on planet earth. Insult has been added to injury, and the unthinkable has happened. The human race has hearkened to the voice of the tempter. Yet in spite of their corruption, they are rapidly swelling their ranks through much procreative activity with Eve's "beautiful" daughters and granddaughters.[7] Children are being born everywhere, speckling the earth with more sons and daughters who have more children. But "be fruitful and multiply" seems to be the only divine command that man obeys. Otherwise, he is in a state of habitual rebellion. "The Lord saw that the wickedness of man was great on the earth, and that every intent of the thoughts of his heart was only evil continually. And the Lord was sorry. .... 'I will blot out man whom I have created,'" God sighs in frustration (Genesis 6:5–7).

We all know the urge to abandon lost causes—projects, relationships and investments that are not giving the expected return. Yet for God, who created man, this urge to destroy conflicts with the essence of His life-giving nature. He cannot follow through without more protracted effort to save. He speaks to the one who has "found favor," the righteous Noah, who "walked with God" (Genesis 6:8, 9). In this family of eight is the one pocket of righteousness remaining. "Make for yourself an ark of gopher wood," God says, giving detailed instructions for building a tri-level, sink-proof vessel that will house a sampling of every living creature on the planet (v.14).[8] For 120 years Noah prophesies with his voice and with his hammer, to the tune of incredulous scoffing. No one is converted. After suffering long with a wicked, unbelieving people, God turns a corner. A century before, He had overlooked their folly, for "the times of this ignorance God winked at;" but once they had been fully warned, He "command[ed] all men everywhere to repent" (Acts 17:30 KJV). When they didn't, God responded accordingly. With Noah's last hammer stroke, He stopped winking.

At God's bidding, Noah's family boards the ark along with a sampling of creatures of every sort. The hatchway of the ark is shut, and "the fountains of the great deep burst open, and the floodgates of the sky" (Genesis 7:11). Nature is driven from her placid course by a supernatural hand. Water bursts from the earth in powerful jets, meeting cascades of water that pour from the heavens. Rivers overflow their boundaries, rushing in torrents that rise higher and higher to engulf the land and its wailing inhabitants. Violent wind hurls natural and man-made structures in every direction, until finally the entire land mass is swallowed up in the wild, indifferent waters. Only Noah and his family of eight are left to repopulate the earth.

SODOM AND GOMORRAH

Scroll forward four centuries. Follow Noah's lineage through his son Shem for nine generations to the wizened, weathered centurion Abraham. He has just entertained three celestial visitors, one of whom is "the Lord," who promises, "at the appointed time I will return to you, at this time next year" (Genesis 18). Then comes the unbelievable good news—"Sarah shall have a son" (v. 14). Along with this joyful assurance, Abraham receives a message of doom: Sodom is about to be judged for its wickedness. Unfortunately, Abraham's nephew Lot is a respected figure in the lush, opulent city. Abraham bargains with God, asking, "Suppose there are fifty righteous within the city; wilt Thou indeed sweep it away?" (Genesis 18:24). The patriarch affirms the principles of divine justice when he answers his own question: "Far be it from Thee to do such a thing, to slay the righteous with the wicked, so that the righteous and the wicked are treated alike. ... Shall not the Judge of all the earth deal justly?" (Genesis 18:25). God affirms Abraham's assumption; if there are only fifty, He will spare the city.

The stakes get higher as the numbers get lower. What about forty, God? What about thirty? Twenty? Ten? With each increment, the answer is the same—God will not destroy the city if there are even ten righteous in it. The problem is that there are fewer than ten. Lot's family alone, and barely they, are the only souls in that vast place who can even tentatively merit the label "righteous." The rest are, morally speaking, pond scum. God moves to Plan B: When the number of godly people is small enough, evacuate them. Instead of sparing the city, He will evacuate the righteous. Then He will wipe the place out.

The angels visit Lot. Notice that there are two who venture into Sodom, while there were three who visited Abraham.

This is because God Himself was one of the "angels" meeting with Abraham. He then sent the two angels alone into Sodom. God in His omniscience knew that the city was beyond salvage, but perhaps He wished for His heavenly comrades to see its state with their own eyes.

And see it they did. Lot met the strangers in the town square and invited them home for the night. When they expressed the desire to stay in the square, Lot begged them to accompany him home. He well knew the character of the local citizenry. Once home, a surprise visit from a group of local thugs confirmed Lot's worst nightmares. They demanded the surrender of his houseguests, stating their intention to rape them.[9]

Lot walked out the front door and closed it behind him. When the argument that ensued almost cost him his life, the angels inside summoned their superhuman powers and struck the perverts blind. One would think this would sober them, but these men were so imbued with evil that they continued to grope for the door. Inside, the angels got down to business with their host. Warning Lot of the imminent destruction of the city, they implored him, in turn, to warn his loved ones. This prompted Lot to attempt to enlist his sons-in-law and married daughters, but to no avail. At sunrise, the angels grasped the hesitant Lot, his two daughters, and his wife, and led them outside the city.

"Then the Lord rained on Sodom and Gomorrah brimstone and fire from the Lord out of heaven, and He overthrew those cities, and all the valley, and all the inhabitants of the cities, and what grew on the ground" (Genesis 19:24, 25).

In case we wonder who the source of this incinerating sulfur was, we are told no less than three times in the space of one sentence; "*the Lord* rained on Sodom and Gomorrah brimstone and fire *from the Lord out of heaven.*" Because of a divinely directed catastrophe, Sodom and Gomorrah were little more than an ash scar on the south side of the Dead

Sea. The only rebel that wasn't turned to ashes was turned to salt. Only when the fire had burned all there was to burn did it die.

The Exodus

One more important judgment occurred 400 years later.[10] The oppressors of God's people had exhausted the limits of His forbearance in the country of Egypt, where God's people were enslaved. Through the partial judgments of the ten plagues, God attempted to turn Pharaoh from his obstinate course. The Nile turned to blood, and pests of every stripe overran the country. Farm animals dropped dead and the people's skin festered into boils. Tree-shattering hail fell and darkness enveloped the land. Through all these national emergencies, the arrogant monarch wavered between deluded pride and fearful submission. Finally, holding the limp body of his first-born son, the king sobbed to Moses, "Rise up, get out from among my people, both you and the sons of Israel; and go, worship the Lord, as you have said. Take both your flocks and your herds, as you have said, and go, and bless me also" (Exodus 12:31, 32).

But rebellion is like a cancer that can be beaten into dormancy by strong medicine, only to spring forth later with a vengeance. Before Pharaoh's tears had fully dried, the pain of bereavement was consumed by his unquenchable desire for dominance. His 2 million slaves and his arch nemesis Moses would come back to Egypt and resume their toils, he vowed. God even accommodated Pharaoh's boldness by leading the freed slaves to the Red Sea, where they were apparently shut in and an easy prey.[11] In this way, God dammed up the flow of human help that He might manifest His own power. Pharaoh forgot about that power and followed hard on Moses' trail.

A formidable army thundered across the desert after the people of God. With few weapons and no military training, the Hebrews were no match for Pharaoh's 600-plus chariots—enough to wipe them out many times over. Just as the army closed in, however, the pillar of cloud that had served as a beacon for the hordes traveled around them and interposed itself between Pharaoh and his prey. It blazed on the Hebrew side, illuminating their path, while on the Egyptian side it created a wall of darkness that stayed their progress.

> "Then Moses stretched out his hand over the sea; and the Lord swept the sea back by a strong east wind all night, and turned the sea into dry land, so the waters were divided" (Exodus 14:21).

While the massive walls of water hovered, the sons of Israel walked all night on an impossibly dry ocean floor. Like animals driven by blind instinct, incorrigible Egyptians set out after them. But as morning kissed the earth and the feet of Israel touched the eastern shore, the elements lashed out at the pursuers. Rain pelted. Wind whipped. Thunder pealed and lightning flashed. The earth trembled. Amidst the confusion, the chariot wheels of Egypt swerved out of their course, prompting memories of God's power to devastate human schemes. Suddenly they knew that God was fighting for the Hebrews and fighting against them. Before panic could dictate a change of course, Moses stretched out his rod over the waters, and their immeasurable volumes obediently rolled back, swallowing Pharaoh and his drones into their killing depths.

FINDING A MOTIVE

The first three destructive judgments of the Bible—the Flood, Sodom and Gomorrah, and the Red Sea—are some of the most direct and forceful accounts of God's retribution. On the intrinsic/extrinsic spectrum, they plot hard on the extrinsic extreme. While some argue that these occurrences were mere natural disasters that God capitalized on, calling them His own, the Bible does not present the matter this way.[12] God Himself is given full credit for these supernatural phenomena. Yet these seemingly aggressive, destructive acts issued forth from a heart of love. While the divine source of these retributive acts can't be denied, we must recognize that they are set apart from human vengeance. When God takes action against an enemy, it is with principles in place that have but a faint reflection in humanity. Here are a few of the identifying characteristics of God's acts of justice:

Infinite Love: The primary distinguishing factor between God's pure wrath and human retaliation is the underlying motive. In the case of human revenge, there is always some element of self-seeking. But when God vindicates Himself, He is not merely defending Himself as an individual. As the keeper and source of all life, He is defending life itself. When the sustainer ensures His own existence, He assures the sustenance of those who depend upon Him. "In Him we live and move and exist" (Acts 17:28). To allow His government to crumble would be to allow all creation, which depends upon His righteous and benevolent rule, to crumble with Him. At the heart of God's white-hot anger against sin and its chaos is a fatherly protectiveness toward the order of the cosmos and every being that is made safe by that order.

Unlike human military conquerors, God *loves* His enemies. Love for the enemy motivates even His acts of destruction. The decision to drop the A-bomb on Hiroshima and Nagasaki might have been made out of a desire to end World War II, but can it be said that it was out of *love* for the nearly 200,000 dead Japanese as well? In the broadest sense, all human beings are God's people. Agape mandates that the eternal welfare of each and every soul be considered before any life is taken. When God "drops a bomb," be it through flood or fire or mighty sea, He does it out of love for each person destroyed as well as each person saved. He covets the compassionate and fair treatment of every soul, although sometimes this involves taking life. How can this be so?

Infinite Knowledge: There is a point, a point that only omniscience can identify, when a person is better off dead than alive. When God all-knowingly sees that the point of no return has been reached, and that the soul is absolutely hardened in rebellion, He sometimes mercifully takes away the life that would only result in the compiling of further guilt and punishment. The antediluvians, the inhabitants of Sodom, and Pharaoh's army, had sealed their hearts in defiance of heaven. If allowed to live, they would do nothing but add to their own future tribulation. It was an act of mercy on God's part that cut their existence short.

Infinite Precision: Scroll back once more to the Exodus for an insight into how divine judgments are decided—not according to arbitrary decrees or impulsive outbursts, but according to fixed laws of retributive justice. After extending multiple warnings and invitations to repent of their cruelty and oppression, God began executing a series of carefully conceived "surgical strikes" against the Egyptian people, their economy, and their idolatrous belief system. Gradually ratcheting up the level of severity from tolerable hardship to outright devastation, all the while extending offers of mercy, the Lord systematically deprived the Egyptians of all they had immorally gained through centuries of exploitation. The punishment fit the crime in a way that only an infinite intelligence could conceive, and the Egyptians couldn't help but comprehend. In the end, Pharaoh and his minions paid with their lives for draining away the life of God's oppressed people.

In the last day, the sin that the lost cherish will be recompensed by God Himself. Yet this event will not be fueled by retaliatory passion or impulsive revenge. It will be borne of the need to uphold the principles of justice for the good of all. Far from being random, subjective choice on the part of God, the guilt will lie with the individual for the wrath that is stored up to their account. "But because of your stubbornness and unrepentant heart *you are storing up wrath for yourself* in the day of wrath and revelation of the righteous judgment of God, who will render to every man according to his deeds" (Romans 2:5, 6, emphasis supplied).

Infinite Justice: Some understand the need for God to exterminate the wicked, but cringe at the thought of punishment. Why must there be suffering proportionate to the suffering caused? Can't God just pull the plug? For many whose lives have had little negative impact, this will indeed be the case. But for those who have inflicted great harm, justice demands that they feel and experience what they caused others to undergo. Paul told the persecuted believers of Thessalonica: "For after all it is only just for God to repay with affliction those who afflict you" (2 Thessalonians 1:6). John echoes this sentiment, addressing the great beast power at the end of the ages: "If anyone is destined for captivity, to captivity he goes; if anyone kills with the sword, with the sword he must be killed" (Revelation 13:10). It is "only just" that one who causes harm be harmed. It "must" be that one who persistently enslaves and kills be enslaved and killed. If justice were to flinch in the face of these demands, its entire structure would be destroyed, and anarchy would ravage the universe. The foundation of life itself rests upon the law of God. No form of life could be supported in a universe where that law was compromised in any way.

Infinite Mercy: To the untrained eye, this raw justice appears out of sync with the character of a loving God. It seems cruelly impersonal. That's because it is only half of the love equation. As much as justice demands punishment and death of the guilty one, mercy requires that the guilty one be given salvation, even at infinite cost. Theologian Frank Hasel states, "The good news of the Bible is not that there is no wrath of God, but that humankind is saved from wrath through faith in Jesus Christ."[13] While God could not change His law, He could send Jesus to meet its demands. This act of compassionate self-sacrifice will remain unrivaled for endless ages. It sweeps away all accusations that the righteous government of God reveals a self-centered, exacting autocrat. It will ever stand as a monument, both of God's unwavering justice and His audacious mercy. "For what the Law could not do, weak as it was through the flesh, God did: sending His own Son in the likeness of sinful flesh" (Romans 8:3). The justice of God alone cannot save. It is His justice coupled with mercy that comprises the love that emptied heaven in order to redeem the world.

Endnotes

1. Richard Rhodes, *The Making of the Atomic Bomb* (New York, Simon & Schuster, 1986), p. 728.

2. Keiko Sasaki, 6 years old in 1945, from A-Bomb WWW Museum, at http://www.csi.ad.jp/ABOMB/children.html

3. David Grossman, "Trained to Kill," *Christianity Today*, August 10, 1998.

4. The "Lawgiver and Judge" is the "One who is able to save and to destroy" (James 4:12). The One who had intimate dealings with Israel, guiding and disciplining them through the desert was Jesus Christ (See 1 Corinthians 10:4).

5. 2 Peter 2:4–6 and Jude 5–7 are parallel passages that together speak of four judgments; Lucifer's expulsion from heaven, the Flood, the Red Sea, and Sodom and Gomorrah. The 2 Peter passage mentions the fallen angels, the Flood, and Sodom and Gomorrah. The Jude passage does not mention the Flood, but mentions the destruction of the Egyptians at the Red Sea.

6. Matthew 25:41.

7. See Genesis 6:2.

8. See Genesis 6:14–16.

9. See Genesis 19:4, 5.

10. Abraham was 75 years old when he received the covenant and left Haran (Genesis 12:4). He had Isaac just after the destruction of Sodom at 100 years of age (Genesis 21:5). Paul says that there were 430 years from Abraham's covenant to Sinai (Galatians 3:17).

11. See Exodus 14:1, 2.

12. "The miracles by which God has from time to time intervened in the ordinary process of nature generally consist in the use of existing natural forces and elements in an unusual manner." *Seventh-day Adventist Bible Commentary* (Hagerstown, MD: Review and Herald Publishing, 1978), Vol. 1, p. 335.

13. Frank Hasel, "The Wrath of God," *Ministry*, November, 1991.

Chapter Eleven

With God on Our Side

dams County, Ohio, 1997. The last strokes of paint were laid on four spanking-new high school buildings, and a shining granite monument of the Ten Commandments was placed in each of the four schoolyards, next to the flagpole.[1] To the local Christians of patriotic bent, it was a pristine picture of a blissful marriage between God and country.

About a year later, an angry local man wrote several letters to the superintendent of the school district. He proposed the placement of some other monuments, saying he wanted equal exposure for his own religious group, called "The Center for Phallic Worship." The request was ignored. Half a year later, the American Civil Liberties Union filed a suit demanding the removal of the Ten Commandment monuments. The suit named the entire school board, as well as the superintendent, as defendants. The plaintiff was Barry Baker, the interim director for the Center for Phallic Worship.

A rally was held two days later at a local church in Peebles, Ohio, with 600 in attendance and standing room only. Supporters at the rally said it was "small town America at its best: a grassroots movement that is part patriotic rally, part revival."[2] This was the beginning of what has become a protracted battle between a citizens group called the "Adams County for the Ten Commandments" (ACTC) and their phallic-worshiping enemies. The ACTC began to order and distribute blue and white yard signs that displayed the Ten Commandments with the legend "We Stand for the Ten Commandments" at the top. They also continued to hold rallies, one of which featured author Peter Marshall, who "emphasized the fallacy of the so-called 'separation of church and state' that has guided Supreme Court rulings for the past fifty years."[3] By October of 2002, the movement had gained enough momentum to distribute 170,000 of the blue and white signs.[4]

The ACTC story has become one of many symbolic battles in America's cultural war between the religious right and secular humanism. Such religiously influenced groups take up legal and political arms against their enemies, often using a rhetoric that couples Christianity with American patriotism as if the two are conjoined twins. It was innocent enough that the citizens of Adams County desired to honor the Ten Commandments, but when some called the separation of church and state a "fallacy," a certain chill entered the air. Yet these sentiments are more common than we think. The most radical of religious patriots advocate complete dissolution of the wall of separation. Consider this statement by reconstructionist Gary North: "We must use the doctrine of religious liberty to gain independence for Christian schools until we train up a generation of people who know that there is no religious neutrality. ... Then they will get busy in constructing a Bible-based, political, and religious order which finally *denies the religious liberty of the enemies of God.*"[5]

Human beings have a history of legislating religion. When a state religion is formed, it is typically imposed upon other nations. Holy war is the natural outcome of the notion that one's country has God's indiscriminate blessing upon its political causes. Although the early Christian church advocated pacifism—with such illustrious figures as Tertullian and Origen endorsing it—this practice was displaced around the third century A.D. With the church-state fusion of Constantine, the theory of "just war" gained prominence. This theory states that Christians can and should engage in armed combat if the cause is a fair one. This opened the door for more blatantly religious wars. The crusades of the Middle Ages were religio-political conflicts in which Christians sought to take back Jerusalem from the "heathen" Turks. The Inquisition was also the product of a church-state union in which church leaders attempted to systematically destroy all dissenters. Clearly the history of Christendom includes many instances in which religious leaders felt led by God to exterminate their fellow man. What motivated them? And what motivates similar movements today?

Amazingly, a misreading of the Old Testament story.

God's Own State Religion

Coined by the Jewish historian Josephus, the term *theocracy* is derived from two Greek words that mean "rule by the deity." The theocracy of Israel was a church-state union of which God Himself was the unseen head. The laws of that nation legislated religious choices and enforced obedience to religious standards—sometimes under penalty of death.[6] In addition, Israel had a military. God commanded it to enter foreign countries and exterminate their inhabitants. It is in the Bible that we find the first religious crusaders, killing in the name of God. So what is to keep any God-fearing nation today from following suit? Why was theocracy so right then and so wrong now? Don't we have the biblical green light for resurrecting a state religion, and shouldn't it be Christianity?

No. The same God who once stood as civil head of Israel, clearly pronounced its dissolution as a theocracy. Jesus said to the Jewish leaders, "The kingdom of God will be taken away from you, and be given to a nation producing the fruit of it" (Matthew 21:43). Today the Israel of God is a spiritual entity that is defined by faith rather than lineage.[7] In contrast to Israel's previous religio-civil power, the church is invested with strictly spiritual authority. It has jurisdiction over matters of the soul and is to wield that power with mercy proportionate to the privilege. Through prayer it can win battles that cannot be entered into by earthly entities. Through the power of the Spirit working in its midst, it is fitted to engage in a work far more solemn and important than any civil conquest. Jesus recognized this transfer from civil to spiritual power when He said, "My kingdom is not of this world. If My kingdom were of this world, then My servants would be fighting, that I might not be delivered up to the Jews" (John 18:36).

Yet the Jewish theocracy had its place and its purpose. Established by God at a time when the surrounding tribes and nations believed themselves to be ruled by their gods through their priests and monarchs, God ruled Israel through a system of government that was familiar to them and their neighbors. In keeping with His method of working with humanity throughout history, He condescended to relate within the context of the familiar while imbuing it with a dignity and meaning beyond its customary limitations. While "the various deities" of Israel's polytheistic neighbors "were considered as having territorial jurisdiction, fighting for their respective peoples and defending the lands in which they dwelled,"[8] God went a step further—He brazenly declared Himself the one true God, the "God above all gods" (2 Chronicles 2:5 KJV). And it was ever His intention that Israel should be the conduit through whom He would convey this saving knowledge to the surrounding nations.

God had promised Abraham 400 years before, "In you *all* the families of the earth shall be blessed" (Genesis 12:3, emphasis supplied). Abraham's descendants, who had now become as numerous "as the sand of the sea," were to carry out this great commission of blessing (Genesis 32:12). So He prepared them for their crucial role by delivering them from their Egyptian slave masters with a mighty hand, by miraculously providing for their every need, by protecting them from the elements and their hostile neighbors. He strove continually to cultivate within them an awareness of their need of Him, to elevate their minds above the carnal to the spiritual, to impress upon them their incredible privilege in being made progenitors of the Messiah. Yet all His "new covenant" promises and enablings they insisted on translating into "old covenant" do's and don'ts, forcing God to relate to them on the superficial level of reward and punishment. In so doing, they deprived themselves of that which would have enabled them to render true heart obedience and become the channel of blessing they were meant to be.

Straying again and again from their source of strength, Israel eventually rotted from the inside. By the time her Messiah appeared, she was captive to Rome. This backslidden nation proved something that those who would revive theocracy should pay heed to—that cultures cannot be saved unless the individuals that comprise them are saved. Moral rectitude en masse can't come through legislation. After all, if God Himself couldn't enforce pervasive national righteousness, no one can.

Yet in keeping with His redemptive character, God has capitalized on their failure in order to communicate saving truth. In the experiment of ancient Israel, we see the utter impotence of human effort apart from divine help—and we see a parallel of our own faithlessness. Like Israel, we often try to do God's will in our own strength, and we fail miserably. Yet this failure can be the beginning of true, God-powered success. Israel was "kept in custody under the law, being shut up to the faith which was later to be revealed" (Galatians 3:23). Then "when the fulness of the time came, God sent forth His Son"(Galatians 4:4). The light that had glimmered for so long became a hallowed blaze in Jesus Christ. Now God could transport His kingdom from a temporal nation to a spiritual one.

INTRANATIONAL JUDGMENTS

Spiritual Israel still has much to learn from its temporal predecessor. Their experiences are "examples for us ... written for our instruction" (1 Corinthians. 10:6, 11). In the harrowing adventures of the Hebrew people, we see our own trials, triumphs and temptations. With this in mind, let's consider God's judicial dealings with and through His people.

As ex-slaves, the people needed to be awakened to the holiness of God and the solemnity of their mission. Only through His divine power would they succeed in crossing the wilderness into the Promised Land. There was need of internal discipline that the ranks might be purged of the moral decay that would lead to their ruin. From the Exodus to the conquest of Canaan, Israel underwent a boot camp experience through a series of "intranational" judgments— judgments within the nation itself, directed by God Himself. The first instance, the precedent, occurred at Mount Sinai.

After receiving the Ten Commandments, Moses descended from Sinai carrying the stone tablets engraved by the finger of God. A strange, anarchic sound wafted to his ears as he spied the Israelites, sodden with wine and fired with lust, worshiping an icon of their own creating. Moses' angry adrenaline charge was sufficient to enable him to shatter the stone tablets and burn the golden calf to powder. He threw the ashes into the waters that flowed through the plain at the foot of Sinai and forced the rebels to drink. He confronted the spineless Aaron for accommodating the scheme. Finally, when enough time had passed to allow for repentance, the great leader drew a figurative line in the sand. Beckoning all contrite souls to himself, he instructed the Levites—the only tribe who had not joined the collusion—to take the sword to those who remained in rebellion.

We might be tempted to think Moses was having little more than a temper tantrum—after all, he had a police record for rage-driven murder. But Moses had grown since his days as a haughty Egyptian prince. Listen to his conversation with God just before his outburst:

> ***God:***   Let me destroy these people, and I will create a royal dynasty out of you.
>
> ***Moses:***   Oh Lord, how can you be angry with these people you've saved so signally? The Egyptians will gloat if you destroy them, saying that you plotted to kill them all along. Please reconsider. Remember your covenant with Abraham, Isaac and Jacob. You said you would make *them* a great nation.[9]

Then a while later:

> ***Moses:***   This group of people has pulled each other into the abomination of idolatry. But please forgive them—and if you can't, blot my name out of the book of life.[10]

These are not the sentiments of a man on a thoughtless rampage. They are the heart cries of a shepherd who would give his life for the sheep. He would rather have them than national greatness. He would rather die with them than live without them. His anger, his punitive acts, and his implementation of the death sentence were also motivated by selfless care of others. A little careful thinking will reveal how this can be so.

Israel was wandering a vast wilderness, untrained in war, without a fortress, and vulnerable to attack. They were surrounded by cruel, warlike nations that could cut them down in a flash. They could not afford to be without God's protection for a moment. Widespread apostasy would grieve away God's sheltering care and leave them defenseless. The few who would repeatedly seduce the many were a threat to the survival of all. God knew that these few who still stood there in haughty defiance were intractable. And so in mercy to them and their potential victims He ordered the death sentence.

Many more of what might be called "intranational" judgments followed over the next 40 years while Israel passed through a prolonged adolescence. In fact, it wasn't until the invasion of Canaan that God again brought judgment to unbelievers. Throughout the wandering years, God restricted His punitive measures to His own people. He was not, and is not, partial. He could not use Israel as a channel of justice unless Israel itself first endured divine discipline. Rich in lessons of Christian accountability, these judgments, inflicted within the borders of the camp, speak to spiritual Israel. Here are some of their characteristics:

Bathed in Prayer. Moses and Aaron played mediatorial roles during the times of divine retribution when it often seemed as though God was against Israel, and Moses and Aaron were for them. Yet it was the Spirit of God who filled His servants and affected this intercessory posture that would later find its richest expression in Jesus Christ. In these instances, Jehovah reflected the holiness and justice of God while Moses and Aaron reflected His nearness and mercy. In a beautiful and illustrative way, there was intimate teamwork between God and His human partners. The sentencing of Israel was not a unilateral process, but a joint effort between the representative of the law and the representatives of the people.

Full of Warning. When the mutinous few had hardened themselves beyond hope, their demise served as a warning to those who were not yet hopeless. This aspect of judgment is called "deterrence," because witnessing the net effect of sin often deters sin in those watching. In observing the severity of God's response to evil, our sin-dulled perceptions are re-tuned and instructed in righteousness. "Then all the people will hear and be afraid, and will not act presumptuously again" (Deuteronomy 17:13).

This principle of deterrence was seen when Korah, Dathan, and Abiram carried out their coup against the leadership of Moses. In response to the mass seduction they instigated, a signal judgment came from God. These lawless libertines were literally swallowed up by the earth along with all they possessed. Some time elapsed after this to give the 250 princes, who had been swept up in Korah's flattery, a chance to recover from its effect. Seeing their charismatic leader put down under the hand of God should have broken his spell. Unfortunately, they held to their rebellion and were destroyed by the fire of God's presence, which lashed out and reduced them to ashes.

This event served as a warning to yet another group— the people themselves. Their affections were still tied to Korah and his propaganda. When the earth swallowed him and the fire destroyed his co-conspirators, the people fled in terror to their tents. But the night that should have been passed in solemn reflection was instead filled with bitter brooding. With the morning light came the accusation to Moses and Aaron, "You have killed the people of the Lord" (Numbers 16:41 NKJV). In spite of the mediation of Aaron, 14,700 of these hardened ones died in a third judgment, bringing the death toll to nearly 15,000.

There was another sector of people warned by these judgments. The camp of Israel was positioned in the middle of an unwalled wilderness, open to the observation of the surrounding nations. News traveled fast from one people to another. Like Exhibit A in God's laboratory, Israel gave perpetual evidence to the idolatrous tribes that there was a God who ruled in the heavens and was powerful in behalf of His people. Yet, if God had only dealt with the sins of their enemies and had indulged the sins of His own children, He might have been seen as their own personal pet deity. The judgments that fell on Jehovah's own people introduced to the pagan nations the idea of an impartial sovereign who ruled over all.

Rich in Mercy. Capital punishment may at times be inhumane in a human court, but when it is God-ordered, one can always know that it is the kindest choice. As noted previously, there are some who, if allowed to live, would only add to their guilt and punishment. God knows when the soul has reached this point of no return, and when He has the authority to then take away the life that would only be used for destructive purposes.

True, some follow this logic and bomb abortion clinics. But the problem with their thinking is that they, in their finite knowledge, do not know when the point of irreversibility is reached, nor do they have the authority to take life. They take upon themselves an office that only God can carry out. And this is the essential flaw in the thinking of those who would initiate a neo-theocracy. They desire to enforce submission to God while they themselves actually usurp His office, trying to bring about a church-state union when He Himself has clearly indicated it should not exist until He comes again.

INTERNATIONAL JUDGMENTS

After 40 years in the crucible, the children of Israel were finally prepared to invade and conquer Canaan. Beginning with the destruction of Jericho, God again began to judge His enemies, this time through His human instruments. There is no way to soften the fact that this was divinely commanded genocide.

> "In the cities of these peoples that the Lord your God is giving you as an inheritance, you shall not leave alive anything that breathes. But you shall utterly destroy them, the Hittite and the Amorite, the Canaanite and the Perizzite, the Hivite and the

Jebusite, as the Lord your God has commanded you"
(Deuteronomy 20:16–17).

This mandate might represent the most difficult rub of
all in the discussion of the principles of divine sovereignty.
How could a God of love command the destruction of entire
nations—men, women and children—by other human beings
who possessed the same sinful nature? How could He initiate
the destruction of sinners by other sinners, when all sinners
are worthy of condemnation? In the words of scholar Ronald
Goetz, "Manifestly, Israel is being helped *in spite* of her sins,
while the Canaanites are being destroyed *because* of theirs."[11]

But the difference in God's treatment of Israel and Canaan
arose because of their respective choices. While Canaan had
filled its cup of iniquity, Israel had not. Speaking with utter
impartiality, God warned Israel:

> "All these things were done by the people who lived
> in the land before you, and the land became defiled.
> And if you defile the land, *it will vomit you out* as
> it vomited out the nations that were before you"
> (Leviticus 18:27, 28 NIV, emphasis supplied).

Don't think yourselves immune, God was saying; the same
rules apply to you. The conquest of Canaan was primarily a
cleansing of sin from a land that was "vomiting" it out. The
sinners within it were purged out because they clung to those
sins. Clinging to those same sins would eventually lead to
Israel meeting the same fate.

Yet the destruction of these individuals along with their
sins does not represent God's original plan for them. Four
hundred years before, God had put them in contact with
Abraham and his vibrant, believable witness of the true God.
Through the patriarch, a lifeline was cast to these peoples.
God explicitly gave Abraham the reason for this effort: "The
iniquity of the Amorite is not yet complete" (Genesis 15:16).

It's as if God were saying, "You will take possession of this land, but not yet, because there's still a chance these people will turn to Me." In fact, God did save Rahab and her family from Jericho.

After beating back the overtures of conscience for four centuries, Canaan had reached the point of intractability. With hearts cauterized by sin, they had developed fully in their specious evils, which included bestiality, child sacrifice, homosexuality, and cult prostitution.[12] The most offensive to God were child sacrifice and public sex rituals: "Are you not children of rebellion, Offspring of deceit, Who inflame yourselves among the oaks, Under every luxuriant tree, Who slaughter the children in the ravines, Under the clefts of the crags?" (Isaiah 57:4, 5). One scholar extrapolates:

> "Pagans practiced 'sympathetic magic'—that is, they believed they could influence the gods' actions by performing the behavior they wished the gods to demonstrate. Believing the sexual union of Baal and Asherah produced fertility, their worshipers engaged in immoral sex to cause the gods to join together, ensuring the good harvests."[13]

Perhaps it was the surplus of babies produced in these orgies that contributed to the practice of child sacrifice. The primary motive, however, was a twisted concept of God that led the people to see Him as a deity that could be appeased and delighted by death:

> "At times of crisis, Baal's followers sacrificed their children, apparently the firstborn of the community, to gain personal prosperity."[14]

Some report that the iron idols were heated with fire, and the tender babes were placed in their searing arms. As the babies cried out in agony, the parents would drown their screams with hymns of praise to Baal. If only these tribes had learned of the benevolent rulership of Jehovah, who would give His own Son rather than require theirs!

There comes a point when God can't forbear with an exploitive people. Mercy toward them equates to cruelty toward those they are exploiting. In His far-reaching wisdom, God knew that the Canaanites as a people would never change. In living they would only add to their own guilt and heap misery upon their victims. Using His own people as the arm of His justice, He made a bold and unmistakable statement. The followers of Jehovah would never be able to deny the consequences of Canaan's sin, for they were instrumental in bringing them. This factor would provide an ongoing reality check for Israel, who would be tempted with the same evils.

Upon entering Canaan, Israel was in special danger of partaking of Baal rites. The farmers among them had long since died off, and these nomadic people lacked confidence in their agricultural abilities. Would God sustain them in their new lives, or should they worship the established local deities? Add to the instinct to survive the lure of illicit, conscienceless sex, and you have a near-perfect formula for spiritual disaster. The only way the people of God would survive the test would be to take a rigidly firm stand against the popular practices of the day. When the people drove out the Canaanite tribes at the command of God, they were to simultaneously drive out the sin these people had come to personify. In implementing the death sentence at the command of God, the Israelites were to express heaven-born antipathy to the vulgar and cruel practices that characterized these warlike tribes.

But just as the Israelites never drove their enemies out of their land, they never drove them completely out of their hearts. They themselves cherished the sins that had ruined the Canaanites, and in so doing brought themselves to eventual ruin. In the history of theocratic Israel, we see clearly a lesson of which today's reconstructionists should take note: The ultimate battle is for the heart. No sword, spear, bomb, or political lobby can achieve victory on that battlefield. It must be conquered by the devastating violence of God's grace. Though God ordained it when all other measures failed, the external imposition of righteousness proved insufficient to conquer the land. How presumptuous, then, to try to reinstate theocracy today, when God Himself has said its era has ceased?

Endnotes

1. This project was initiated by the Adams County Ministerial Association and permitted by the Adams County School Board.

2. ACTC web page, under "Saga", p. 2 http://www.4the10.net/saga_1.htm

3. *Ibid.*, p. 3.

4. *Ibid.*, p. 7.

5. Gary North, Institute for Christian Economics, quoted in Bill Moyer's "God and Politics," PBS, 1987, emphasis supplied.

6. See Exodus 19:13; Leviticus 18:29; 20:27; 24:23; Numbers 15:35; etc.

7. "Neither are they all children because they are Abraham's descendants, but: 'Through Isaac your descendants will be named.' That is, it is not the children of the flesh who are children of God, but the children of the promise are regarded as descendants" (Romans 9:7, 8). "You also, as living stones, are being built up as a spiritual house for a holy priesthood, to offer up spiritual sacrifices, acceptable to God through Jesus Christ" (1 Peter 2:5).

8. "Theology" article, from *New Advent Catholic Encyclopedia,* http://www.newadvent.org/cathen/14568a.htm

9. See Exodus 32:10–13.

10. See Exodus 32:31, 32.

11. Ronald Goetz, *Theology Today,* Vol. 32, No. 3, Oct. 1975, "Joshua, Calvin and Genocide."

12. See Leviticus 18:21–30; 20:23; Deuteronomy 20:16–18; Numbers 25:1–11; Psalm 106:28.

13. Ray Vanderlaan, "That the World May Know—Study Guide II" *Focus on the Family,* 1996.

14. *Ibid.*

Chapter Twelve

The Hammer of the Whole Earth

"With unerring accuracy the Infinite One still keeps account with the nations. While His mercy is tendered, with calls to repentance, this account remains open; but when the figures reach a certain amount which God has fixed, the ministry of His wrath begins. The account is closed. Divine patience ceases. Mercy no longer pleads in their behalf."

—Ellen G. White, *Prophets and Kings* [1]

Of all the ways that God "does" judgment, national judgments executed through hostile human agencies would seem to register most ambiguously on the "intrinsic-extrinsic continuum." Part reaping of natural consequences, part divine "giving up," part indirect application of divine discipline, and nonspecific as to individual guilt, this, of all the types of judgment, strikes us as the most baffling. Yet it was the method God most often used with Israel following their wilderness wanderings.

When Joshua and the members of his generation died, "another generation arose" who "forsook the Lord God of their fathers" and "followed other gods from among … the people who were all around them" (Judges 2:10–12). God's solution was to remove His protective hedge and deliver "them into the hands of plunderers who despoiled them," then to raise "up judges who delivered them" when they repented (vs. 14, 16). Meant to function as a learning experience out of which God hoped His people would mature, it became a permanent arrangement by default. Three hundred twenty-five years later,[2] by the end of the Book of Judges, the Israelites were still stuck in this reward-and-punishment mind-set, hands tightly clenched on the bottom rung of Kohlberg's Stages of Moral Development. As the Philistine war machine pounded them to a quivering mass, instead of committing themselves fully into the care of God, they "added to all [their] other sins the evil of asking for a king" (1 Samuel 12:19 NIV).

It didn't need to be that way. Throughout the Book of Judges, we catch glimpses of what might have been had the early Israelites valued and internalized the comprehensive moral principles enshrined in the Mosaic code, which, according to historian Paul Johnson, constituted "a primitive declaration of equality."[3] Rooted in this egalitarian ethic, many of the stories of Judges portray an "Israelite tradition, already strongly entrenched, of equality, [and] communal discussion"—the hallmarks of an "essentially democratic and meritocratic … society," in which "charismatic heroes, most of whom are low-born, [obtain] advancement through their own energy and abilities, which are brought out by divine favour and nomination."[4]

Yet while the divine provision was sufficient to transform this rustic, semi-cohesive tribal confederacy into a coordinated community of mature believers, and God's channel of blessing for the world, the promise was too often thwarted by human perversity. Liberty became license, freedom gave way to anarchy, and the window of "democratic and meritocratic" opportunity passed. Estranged from God and overwhelmed by fear of their formidable enemies, Israel placed their confidence in a king. God knew how badly their confidence was misplaced, yet He condescended to work within the parameters of their limited understanding and adopted "the concepts of kingship in spite of its flaws."[5]

The Royal Road to Perdition

Chief among those flaws was that, in setting up a king, the people were abdicating their corporate responsibility to a single individual who now "represents [them] before God. And the behavior of that king, in a sense, stands for the whole people. ... The Deuteronomic covenant blesses or curses the nation's obedience or disobedience. Now, suddenly, one person has the power to undo the whole thing. If that one person decides to be evil, the whole nation suffers."[6]

It was an arrangement the nation would learn to regret. Yet flawed as it was, at the people's insistence God condescended to adopt it. And He condescended to inaugurate it with just the sort of larger-than-life, Hollywood action hero any red-blooded Israelite would have chosen if given the chance. But while the strapping young Saul won the admiration of his countrymen for his Herculean stature and dashing exploits, his once humble ego inflated until he spiraled into megalomaniacal madness, and finally death. In place of Saul, a king after the people's own heart, God chose David, "a man after *His* own heart" (1 Samuel 13:14, emphasis supplied). A deeply spiritual man, David "seems to have been much more conscious of the nature of the Israelite religion and community than either Saul or any of his own successors. ... He grasped that it was indeed a theocracy and not a normal state. Hence the king could never be an absolute ruler on the usual oriental pattern."[7]

Recognizing God's absolute authority over His people, David (generally) maintained the attitude of a humble servant, and under his reign the kingdom flourished. For all its domestic intrigues and political crises, the ever-repentant David was able to hand his son, Solomon, a kingdom that was poised to become what God had always meant for it to be—"a light to the Gentiles" in whom "all the families of the earth shall be blessed" (Isaiah 49:6; Genesis 12:3). But while Solomon was granted every inducement and advantage to bring this about, he lost sight of the vision. Abandoning himself to the grossest sin and sensuality, he wasted the privileges, resources and lives with which God had entrusted him. While his eventual repentance secured his own salvation, he had done irreparable damage to his people's confidence in him. Following his death, when it became clear that his son Rehoboam would follow in his tyrannical footsteps, the northern ten tribes bolted from the confederacy, never to return. Ever after, the divided kingdom became a living symbol of the people's divided hearts. And God was placed in the unenviable position of continually trying to win them back—sometimes by speaking softly, sometimes by carrying a big stick.

LET JUSTICE RUN DOWN LIKE WATER

From the start, the northern kingdom of Israel was a spiritual basket case. Following the lead of Jereboam, their rebel king, the majority of the people seem to have hurled themselves into idolatry with reckless abandon. As the priests, Levites and those who "set their heart to seek the Lord God" fled to the still semi-devout southern kingdom of Judah, those who were left resurrected the insidious calf worship for which 3,000 of them had been put to death at Sinai (2 Chronicles 11:16). Yet even while the nation slid down the slippery slope of spiritual and moral debasement, it outstripped its southern neighbor in material prosperity.

Paradoxically, the northern kingdom enjoyed some of its greatest prosperity during the reign of its most wicked king, Ahab. A gifted general and administrator and an ambitious builder, Ahab was nevertheless a morally weak and vacillating character who "did more to provoke the Lord God of Israel to anger than all the kings of Israel who were before him" (1 Kings 16:33). Primarily, he provoked God by importing, through his political marriage to Jezebel, daughter of the king of Sidon, the degrading and seductively sensual worship of Baal, the Canaanite god of thunder and lightning.

An amorous, dynamic figure, Baal was conceptualized as a dashing young warrior "who rode upon the clouds of heaven and hurled lightning from the skies to bring the life-giving rain to the parched earth."[8] In the sun-drenched, drought-prone Near East, fear of famine was ever on the minds of its hand-to-mouth inhabitants. Powerfully motivated by fear on the one hand, and the lure of forbidden pleasure on the other, the Israelites surrendered themselves en masse to the bewitching power of fertility rituals that featured not only illicit sex, but also self-mutilation. Attempting to win Baal's reluctant favor, they "cut themselves ... with knives and lances, until the blood gushed out on them," in seasonal imitation of the Canaanite pantheon, who they imagined "'ploughed' their own flesh and sowed the new corn in readiness for the return of the rains in the autumn" (1 Kings 18:28).[9]

As Jon Paulien has insightfully observed,

"This is animistic thinking: manipulating the gods to keep the rain and the prosperity coming. The Canaanite god Baal was the god of thunder and storm. So he was the deity that provided rain. And the people of the Bible lived in a part of the world that never has enough rain. So if you could get Baal to bring more rain, everything would be great. Thus Israel failed to put God first in the midst of its prosperity. Instead it fell back into primitive ways of relating to God."[10]

Under the influence of this primitive, dehumanizing animism, Israelite culture rapidly deteriorated. Lost were the ennobling principles of justice and equality that God had embedded into the Mosaic code. "Failing to put God first in the midst of its prosperity," Israel blindly pursued prosperity as an end in itself, and inevitably imitated the exploitative policies of its pagan neighbors. Subsequently, "the gap between rich and poor increased. The peasants got into debt, and when they could not pay were expropriated. ... In these circumstances, the prophets re-emerged to voice the social conscience."[11]

And voice it they did, in thunderous indictments. Speaking through the rustic prophet Amos, the Lord delivered this scathing rebuke against the corrupt Israelite glitterati, "Woe to you ... Who cause the seat of violence to come near, Who lie on beds of ivory ... Eat lambs from the flock ... Who drink wine from bowls ... But are not grieved for the affliction of Joseph" (Amos 6:3–6). Utterly disgusted with their greed and hypocrisy, God lamented, "I hate, I despise your feast days, And I do not savor your sacred assemblies. Though you offer Me burnt offerings and your grain offerings, I will not accept them. ... But let *justice* run down like water, And *righteousness* like a mighty stream" (Amos 5:21–24, emphasis supplied).

Such unsparingly straight talk, intertwined with eloquent calls to repentance and impassioned messages of mercy, fell, for the most part, on deaf ears, until Israel's cup of iniquity overflowed with vice and cruelty. Having spent lavishly of His mercy on His prodigal people, the divine accountant saw that continued blessing would only result in continued abuse and exploitation, so He closed the northern kingdom's overdrawn "account." It was time now for the ministry of wrath. Ceasing His pleadings, the advocate sadly declared, "Ephraim is joined to idols; Let him alone," and reluctantly "gave him up" to the judge, who solemnly intoned, "Prepare to meet your God, O Israel!" (Hosea 4:17; Amos 4:12).

THE ROD OF MY ANGER

God facilitated this "meeting" through the medium of the Assyrians, whom He authorized to act as His instruments of judgment. As He later characterized them through the prophet Isaiah, Assyria was "the rod of [His] anger And the staff in whose hand" was God's "indignation." God Himself had given Assyria "charge, To seize the spoil, to take the prey, And to tread [His own people] down like the mire of the streets" (Isaiah 10:5, 6). Fiercely imperialistic and ferociously cruel, Assyria battered the northern kingdom over a period of decades, finally subduing them during the reign of Shalmaneser V, who carried off the Israelite elite, scattered them to the farthest reaches of his kingdom, and displaced them with his own people. "Thus the first great mass tragedy in Jewish history took place. It was, too, a tragedy unrelieved by ultimate rebirth. The holocaust dispersion of the northern people of Israel was final. In taking their last, forced journey into Assyria, the ten tribes of the north moved out of history and into myth."[12]

One might well ask how God could use such a notoriously bloodthirsty nation to execute judgment upon His—or any—people. What kind of justice could possibly be affected by a nation that flayed its captives alive and jubilantly carpeted a victory pillar with their skin?[13] If we are horrified by such wanton cruelty between human beings, the One who made humanity is more so. Yet such is the unavoidably tragic nature of national judgments. As people groups become settled into an irreversible pattern of perversity and oppression, preventing God from engaging them in more constructive avenues, He must both give them over to the intrinsic consequences of their choices, and sovereignly use those consequences as a vehicle through which to apply judicial penalties—correctively for those who will receive it as such, punitively for those who will not. It might even be said that such temporal judgments constitute an encounter with reality, both practically and morally. Still, even in the midst of such judgments, we see mercy, as God delayed the inevitable as long as He could while inviting the repentant to find refuge in the still-intact southern kingdom of Judah.

It's hard to see the fairness in these punishments. Clearly such temporal judgments are not entirely specific as to individual culpability, as "both righteous and wicked" are together "cut off" (Ezekiel 21:3). Again, such is the nature of national judgments, as "the innocent are frequently involved in the same temporal sufferings as the guilty" due to the perversity of their leaders.[14] United under the headship of a king whose behavior represented them, and relationally, culturally and politically enmeshed with one another, the individuals who comprised the nation of Israel were in a certain sense regarded as a single entity by God. Yet while He dissolved their national identity in consequence of their corporate guilt, He continued to relate redemptively to them as individuals.

Still another question arises: How could God punish one nation with another without trampling His own principles of freedom of choice? Were the Assyrians merely the pawns of His irresistible sovereign will, manipulated like so many stringed marionettes? Contradictory as it might seem, their hostility was not inspired by God, nor did He compel them to behave in any way contrary to their will. The Bible provides this fascinating psychological insight: "This is not what [Assyria] intends, this is not what he has in mind; his purpose is to destroy, to put an end to many nations" (Isaiah 10:7 NIV). God did not inspire the Assyrians' hostility; it arose from within their own carnal hearts, but He overruled it for purposes of judgment. And ultimately, He would hold them accountable for their gratuitous brutality. Assyria would, in turn, be chastised through Babylon, whom God would next employ as His instrument of judgment.

The Hammer of the Whole Earth

It's become a familiar pattern by now. When human perversity frustrates the redemptive will of God, He graciously adapts by expressing it through another avenue. While the northern kingdom of Israel had invalidated its divine calling and, subsequently, its national existence, the southern kingdom of Judah had not yet exhausted its probation. For 150 more years,[15] God would plead and chasten, woo and warn His people, trying to instill within them a sense of their high calling as His conduit of truth and the progenitors of the Messiah. There are glimmers of greatness and hope in the reigns of Asa, Jehoshaphat, Joash, Hezekiah, Josiah, and other kings, with many marked and miraculous deliverances from their more powerful enemies. Yet for all of God's redemptive inducements and interventions, Judah's checkered history reveals a kingdom divided against itself.

Plowing through the long, painful litany of royal succession is like watching a relay race being conducted by members of the same team who are intent on racing in opposite directions. For every "good" king who grabbed the baton and ran the race for the glory of God, his equally "evil" son seized it from him only to dash madly the other way. If Hezekiah "removed the high places and broke the sacred pillars" of his idol-worshiping subjects, his dissolute son Manasseh "rebuilt the high places," "raised up altars for Baal ... as Ahab king of Israel had done," and "made his son pass through the fire [of Molech], practiced soothsaying, used witchcraft, and consulted spiritists and mediums" (2 Kings 18:4; 21:3, 6). If Manasseh's even more dissolute son Amon "walked in all the ways that his father had walked; and ... served the idols that his father had served," his devout son Josiah "broke down and pulverized" the altars that his grandfather had erected and "executed all the priests of the high places ... on the altars, and burned men's bones on them" (2 Kings 21:21; 23:12, 20). While the people generally responded in kind throughout all of this kingly reformation and deformation, the love of idolatry was never completely uprooted from their hearts. Secular historical records confirm the biblical history:

> "Other deities were worshipped by the Israelites in Jerusalem right up until the city was destroyed by the Babylonians in 586 B.C. ... the Israelites honored the fertility goddess Asherah, the consort of El, in their Temple in Jerusalem as well as a host of Syrian astral deities; they also took part in the fertility rites of Baal. It was not until the exile to Babylon (597–539 B.C.) that the people of Israel finally decided that Yahweh was the *only* God and that no other deities existed."[16]

As had happened with Israel, the principles and practice of sensualized animism choked out the ennobling principles of justice, mercy, and humility (see Micah 6:8). Judah's love affair with idolatry inevitably led to inequity, elitism and oppression, and loss of spiritual vision. Even as God inspired the prophet Isaiah and others with a mature, inclusive vision of a "sophisticated world faith, to which all humanity can turn for answers,"[17] Judah's sinful self-absorption dwarfed its spiritual perceptions and diminished its moral character. To keep the kingdom from completely collapsing upon itself, for its own sake and for the sake of its Messianic mission, God once again chastened His people through a hostile, unbelieving nation.

From the east, the Babylonian military machine surged. Its first order of business was to crush its archrival, Assyria, and the Egyptians who had come to its aid, which it accomplished at the Battles of Nineveh and Karchemish. It spent the next two decades forcing tiny Judah and its neighbors into total submission, until "the hammer of the whole earth" dominated the entire fertile crescent (Jeremiah 50:23). Trying to spare His people from unnecessary destruction, God pled with them through the prophet Jeremiah not to resist their oppressors but to accept their vassal status. Rejecting such counsel as the basest treason, the Babylonian-appointed King Zedekiah broke his oath of submission and forged a military alliance with Egypt, so infuriating King Nebuchadnezzar that he utterly destroyed the city of Jerusalem, including the illustrious temple of Solomon (Isaiah 36:6). Capturing the fleeing Zedekiah, he marveled, "God is great, who hateth that conduct of thine, and hath brought thee under us."[18] Then he proceeded to slaughter his children in front of him, after which he put out his eyes, "standard punishment for a vassal who broke his oath," and dragged him off to Babylon, a broken man.[19]

So ended nearly 500 years of Jewish monarchy. However, unlike Israel, the inhabitants of Judah were not forever scattered to the four winds, nor was their land colonized by the Babylonians, whose rule was far more humane than that of the Assyrians. Humbled by their captivity, they returned from exile thoroughly cured of idolatry and turned their attention to rebuilding their nation and codifying the Scriptures. Through the painful but loving application of judgment, God had managed to preserve a remnant through whom a knowledge of the truth, and the Messianic lineage, would be preserved.

Endnotes

1. Ellen G. White, *Prophets and Kings* (Mountain View, CA: Pacific Press Publishing Association, 1943), p. 364.

2. See *Nelson's Complete Book of Bible Maps and Charts* (Thomas Nelson Publishers, 1996), pp. 74, 75; Joshua died around 1375 B.C., and Saul was coroneted in about 1050 B.C.

3. Paul Johnson, *A History of the Jews* (New York: Harper Perennial, a division of Harper and Row Publishers, Inc., 1987), p. 40.

4. *Ibid.*, p. 45.

5. Jon Paulien, *Meet God Again for the First Time* (Hagerstown, MD: Review and Herald Publishing Association, 2003), p. 43.

6. *Ibid.*, pp. 43, 44.

7. Johnson, p. 57.

8. Karen Armstrong, *Jerusalem: One City, Three Faiths* (New York: Ballantine Books, 1997), p. 15.

9. Time-Life Books Myth and Mankind Series, *Epics of Early Civilization: Myths of the Ancient Near East,* Myth and Mankind Series (London, UK: Duncan Baird Publishers, 1998), p. 107.

10. Paulien, p. 48.

11. Johnson, p. 66.

12. *Ibid.*, p. 70.

13. See http://ancientneareast.tripod.com/Assyria_Subartu.html

14. *Seventh-day Adventist Bible Commentary* (Washington, D.C.: Review and Herald Publishing Association), Vol. 4, p. 649.

15. Israel was carried off to Assyria in 722 B.C. and Judah was exiled to Babylon in three steps: 605 B.C. (Daniel and friends), 597 B.C. (the craftsmen), 586 B.C. (destruction of the temple).

16. Armstrong, p. 27.

17. Johnson, p. 76.

18. Flavius Josephus, *Complete Works* (Grand Rapids, MI: Kregel Publications, 1981), p. 220. Babylon was also later judged and subdued through the Medes and the Persians.

19. Johnson, p. 78.

Chapter Thirteen

What More Could Love Do?

*I*n his book *Holy War, Holy Peace: How Religion Can Bring Peace to the Middle East,* author Marc Gopin relates a personal experience of walking through Jerusalem's Old City after Jewish extremists had upturned the carts of Arab vendors. Examining the carved figures of Moses and Abraham that had littered the ground, Gopin caught the eye of the Palestinian merchant to whom they belonged. Pointing upward, the merchant asked, "One Father?"

The Diaspora, which began with the Babylonian Exile, had the eventual effect of sprinkling Europe with the people who had to that time clung together in the nation of Judah. Centuries of wandering and fierce persecution awaited all these people without a country.[1] Finally in 1948, the nation of Israel was again established under the auspices of Britain, and Jews the world over went to live in Jerusalem, which Britain had captured from the Turks during World War I.

Today the "City of Peace" is anything but. That embattled segment of the once-fertile crescent has become the hotbed of the most prolonged and seemingly hopeless religio-political conflict of all time. If only baby Isaac and Ishmael, 14 years his senior, had known how long their contentions would smolder! From their loins would come two nations that would war against one another, not only in Israel's conquest of Canaan, but in Israel's current effort to remain established in the Land of Promise. Though they have one father in Abraham, that has not given them one heart and one mind, nor the ability to effect reconciliation.

More desperate than the conflict in the Middle East was the conflict between earth and heaven as a result of sin. The incompatibility between a holy God and sinful man outstrips even that of Jews and Palestinians. This disaccord would have threatened humanity to extinction were it not for heaven's peace accord in Christ.

THE COST OF RECONCILIATION

"God was in Christ reconciling the world to Himself, not counting their trespasses against them" (2 Corinthians 5:19). The effect of the cross was to reconcile the Godhead with estranged humanity, and humanity with God. Reconciliation, in the Greek *katallasso*, means to make something totally other than it was. In the New Testament, it is used to describe the mending of the divine-human relationship. It involves the dissolving of enmity and the bringing together of two sides. It evokes images of handshakes and embraces, the laying aside of swords. Tears dried, amends made, everything about reconciliation sighs serene repose.

But at what cost?

The biblical idea of reconciliation is in sharp contrast to the human idea. We relationally lazy, spiritually shallow beings often desire release from the aggravation of conflict, yet we are seldom willing to make the sacrifices needed to bring about that release at the deepest level. We treat the symptoms of estrangement without addressing the tedious and embarrassing causes. We gloss over our differences, smooth over our conflicts, and for this reason our differences and conflicts never go away. Not so with God. God's kind of reconciliation is no slip-shod attempt at superficial conflict management. It is as universal and eternal as the cross of Calvary itself. But be warned—its method is as offensive as its effect is thorough. In God's system of things (which is the only true system), reconciliation requires *death.* In the absence of this understanding, the cross becomes a very unsavory, bloody, and confusing thing, as do the biblical stories that prefigure it. In the presence of this understanding, however, the cross and all its bloody preludes make perfect sense.

KAPHAR ON JORDAN'S BANKS

One such symbolic event is found in Numbers 25. Israel stood poised on the borders of their earthly paradise, their tedious wilderness passage about to end in triumph. After battling alternately with their God and their own stubborn spirits for 40 years, they were ready to battle their corporeal foes. But they mistook who their greatest foes were. Bracing themselves carefully against sword and spear, they failed to deflect the arrows of sexual and spiritual seduction.

The sorcerer Balaam had learned the hard way that a frontal assault upon Israel was a no-win proposition. Moved by the Moabite king's bribe, he attempted to curse Israel, only to hear his own mouth utter a blessing instead. It was as if God played him like a puppet, speaking heaven's words from his devilish lips.

Hell's Plan A having failed, Plan B was put into motion. The enemy could not break through the ramparts of Israel's protector, but he could turn Israel's almighty protector Himself into their enemy. He could not curse Israel, but he could coax Israel to curse themselves through sin. And so the destroyer resorted to his most successful tactic—if you can't beat 'em, invite 'em to a party.

While Israel awaited God's marching orders, they basked in the best that nature and good fortune had to offer. Positioned to take the Promised Land, they rested in a beautiful valley on the eastern side of the Jordan, where flourished the acacia tree. Among the groves they enjoyed balmy breezes and warm sunshine. But the peaceful surroundings masked a foe more violent than sword or spear. The resident Moabites revered the pagan idol Baal and freely engaged in its licentious worship.[2] Even the names of the various shrines conveyed the degrading nature of the rites.[3] Exposed to the onslaught of suggestive allusions, Israel's shock threshold was lowered with each passing day. While on the banks of the heavenly land, friendship with Moab purveyed the sizzling temptations of hell. Finally, we are told, "The people began to play the harlot with the daughters of Moab" (Numbers 25:1).

"And the Lord was angry against Israel. And the Lord said to Moses, 'Take all the leaders of the people and execute them in broad daylight before the Lord' " (vs. 3, 4). Like a sudden thunderhead darkening a cloudless sky, condemnation rolled over the camp in the form of severe judgments. A plague broke out among the masses of people. In order to make an example of the leaders in rebellion, Moses commanded the elders to slay the leaders in rebellion "in broad daylight" (vs. 4). However, while everywhere the woeful wages of sin evinced the intense displeasure of God, one man remained oblivious. A man of privilege, Prince Zimri of the tribe of Simeon, traipsed through the weeping camp with a heathen princess on his arm. Boasting to his brothers of his voluptuous attainment, he proceeded with her into his bedroom.[4]

This height of defiance was met with bold requital. "Phinehas the son of Eleazar, the son of Aaron the priest, saw it." With holy jealously burning in his breast, unable to forbear the insult to divine holiness, he became God's instrument of retribution. "He arose from the midst of the congregation, and took a spear in his hand; and he went after the man of Israel into the tent, and pierced both of them ... through the body" (Numbers 25:7, 8).

The immediate result was that "the plague on the sons of Israel was checked" (v. 8). As he stood amidst the rubble of 24,000 bodies,[5] Moses heard God's voice in approval of this violent act. The priesthood was confirmed to Phinehas's family line—an honor second to none. Why the reward? "Phinehas the son of Eleazar, the son of Aaron the priest, has turned away my wrath ... and *made atonement* for the sons of Israel" (vs. 11–13, emphasis supplied).

This ever-present Old Testament theme of atonement stems from the Hebrew word *kaphar*. The effect of this "atonement" is to make "at-one" two estranged parties—in this case Israel and their God. Bringing together alienated hearts is a common theme, not only in biblical thought, but also in the annals of secular psychology and politics. The Bible, however, provides the sole true remedy for the alienation that separates souls, because it gets to the root cause of that separation. It is *sin* that introduces an impassable barrier between two hearts and prevents true communion. Like a spiritual blood clot, it blocks the vital, life-giving flow of love from one heart to another. Only the removal of sin can restore that flow and revive the deadened relationship. Unless the remedy for alienation includes this *kaphar*, it is at best shallow and temporary.

Rich in meaning, *kaphar* "conveys the sense of appeasing, cleansing, disannulling, forgiving, pacifying, being merciful, purging and putting off. ... Most of the time the verb is used to 'cover' (hide) sin with the blood of a sacrifice, implying that the sin is wiped away."[6] This wiping away of sin is the mandatory prerequisite for reuniting hearts estranged by sin. We can relate to this price of reconciliation in our own lives. How often are relationships left to die out because some offense is never "destroyed" through confession and repentance? Flaccid attempts are made to smooth over the trouble, but the symptoms reappear again and again. Until the wrong is frankly, specifically acknowledged, a proper sense of shame expressed, and restitution made, the relationship is, like a limb with a blood-stopping tourniquet, doomed to die.

The cleansing metaphor is familiar and even pleasant to us, but the wiping away of sin is a much more tragic process than we might assume. Since sin does not live in the abstract, but is harbored within the heart of a volitional being, only the destruction of that being can bring the destruction, or the wiping away, of sin. "Without shedding of blood there is no forgiveness" (Hebrews 9:22). This is the reason that God's law mandates the death of the sinner. And this is the reason Phinehas "made atonement" when he destroyed the lust-crazed Prince Zimri in the valley of the acacia trees. His hurled spear removed that love-frustrating, life-blocking barrier between God and His people Israel, and in so doing made reconciliation possible.

SOMEBODY HAS TO DIE

We might ask, "If the sinner must die in order to destroy sin, why are we still alive?" This question points to the gospel's most basic and beautiful truth. God has, in His infinite wisdom and love, devised a means whereby the sinner can live through the death of another. As the story of

Phinehas exhibits God's anger at sin, it also reveals that His wrath is "turned away" through the destruction of that sin. In the case of Zimri, the sin was destroyed by the destruction of the person who carried it. But thank God that there was, and is, another option. The story of the gospel builds upon the foundation of God's wrath toward sin and uncovers the reality of sin's transference to the Lamb. All throughout Israel's wilderness wanderings, the people of God had opportunity to see this beautiful truth acted out on a daily basis. As the sinner brought a lamb to the tabernacle and slit the throat of that innocent creature, the erring one was able to grasp the central theme of redemption: God had provided a Lamb to die in the sinner's place.[7] Zimri's brazen rebellion conveyed the fact that he had not found shelter in this Lamb. Of his own choice, he placed himself in the direct path of God's retributive justice.

When faced with the sin of humanity, God could not, in keeping with His law, ignore transgression. But He could forgive that transgression if He absorbed the penalty of it into Himself. In God's government, no mere man could die in place of another. In order to be our substitute, the Messiah must be God, for it was God's holy law that had been transgressed. And so it was determined that God would fulfill His own death decree in Jesus Christ. Because Jesus was Creator, He was qualified to assume responsibility for us as a parent would for a child. But He must go even further in identifying with humanity in its sinful state, for the high priest who would represent His people must, as the Law of Moses specified, be one of them.[8] In keeping with this requirement, Jesus "took upon him the form of a servant," and "became obedient unto death, even the death of the cross" (Philippians 2:7, 8 KJV). "God ... sending His own Son in the likeness of sinful flesh and as an offering for sin ... condemned sin in the flesh" (Romans 8:3).

Jesus is presented in Scripture as the second Adam. Author Jon Paulien sums it up:

"The New Testament understanding of how people get right with God, therefore, is firmly grounded in the fact that Jesus Christ is the new creation, the Second Adam, the image of God. He is the one who undoes the curse that afflicted the human race as a result of Adam's sin. Christ is the one who overcomes at the same point at which Adam failed. Through experiencing the full history of Adam, Jesus redeems it." [9]

Because of Jesus, we need not die. God's pointed and hot wrath, bent like Phinehas' spear to destroy sin, need not destroy us. It has already destroyed us—in principle—through the representative merits of Christ's death, when "our old self was crucified with Him, that our body of sin might be done away with" (Romans 6:6). In the cross, the law of God has achieved closure on the sin problem. It no longer has unfinished business to carry out with us.

Why, oh why, will some still face a judgment of condemnation? Because they, like Prince Zimri, have rejected God's gracious provision in Christ. "For if we go on sinning willfully after receiving the knowledge of the truth, there no longer remains a sacrifice for sins" (Hebrews 10:26). Entrenching themselves in a mindset of self-righteous detachment from heaven's gift, and acting out their mindset as humans always eventually do, the Zimris of the world cling to sin and separate from the Savior. Placing themselves outside of Christ, they stand, of their own perverse choice, in the acid rain of sin's consequences. How can they fault God for the death they themselves chose, even if He is involved in the implementation of the death sentence? How can they blame Him for destroying those He first died to save? In giving Himself to save us from death, what more could love do?

Endnotes

1. While some Jews returned to Judah following the decrees of Cyrus and Darius, the majority preferred to remain in the countries in which they had settled.

2. See, for instance, Isaiah 57:3–10; Ezekiel 23:36–45.

3. See Ellen G. White, *Patriarchs and Prophets* (Mountain View, CA: Pacific Press Publishing Association, 1958), p. 453.

4. The word translated "tent" can mean "inner tent" or "inner room." *Qubbah*, only appears once in the Old Testament, and "is a large, vaulted tent (sleeping compartment or bedchamber, from its arched form); a domed cavity, a pavilion."

5. The Numbers' account says 24,000, while Paul's account in 1 Corinthians 10:8 reports that "twenty-three thousand fell in one day." Regardless of the reason for the disparity, it is a huge number.

6. Lexical Aids to the Old Testament, *The Hebrew-Greek Key Study Bible*, entry 3722.

7. See Genesis 22:8.

8. See Hebrews 2:14–18; 5:1–4.

9. Jon Paulien, *Meet God Again for the First Time* (Hagerstown, MD: Review and Herald Publishing Association, 2003), p. 60.

Chapter Fourteen

Forgive and Forget

R iddled with cancer and rapidly failing, 80-year-old Jack Rosenfeld gathered his three adult children around his deathbed for some heart-searching final words.

"'Right here, right now, in front of me,' he said in a wheezy Godfather-like whisper, 'I want you to look each other in the eye and ask for forgiveness for anything [hurtful] you ever said or did to each other, knowingly or unknowingly. ... I need to know there is peace among my children.'"

Fourteen hours after discharging the burden of his heart, Rosenfeld was dead.

Chastened and inspired by their father's deathbed admonition, Rosenfeld's battling offspring reassessed their problematic relationships and became reconciled through the power of mutual forgiveness. Some time after, Rosenfeld's daughter Karen Roekard related that, whenever she and her siblings were tempted to return to their fractious ways, they recalled their father's words and their decision to forgive and forget, and found strength "to return to the place of Shabbat and *shalom bayit*," or domestic tranquility. It's an experience Roekard recently found to be especially relevant as she prepared for the observance of Yom Kippur, the Jewish Day of Atonement, "a day rooted in the sacred power of self-examination and forgiveness"—and resultant reconciliation.[1]

GOD'S SHOW AND TELL

The Hebrew word *kippur*, atonement, comes from the root *kaphar*, which, as explained in the previous chapter, means to cover or to cancel. Yom Kippur, observed on the tenth day of the month of Tishri[2] and regarded by Jews as the highest holy day of the Jewish year, is a time to experience the cancellation of sins through honest, searing self-examination that results in life-changing *teshuvah*, or repentance. Wrongs are to be made right, and reconciliation with God and fellow beings is to be established. The extensive liturgy includes prayer and personal and corporate confession of sin, the latter at times accompanied by the smiting of the breast, a symbolic gesture of repentance.[3] During the concluding service of the liturgy, the entire congregation remains standing before the open ark, or cabinet, containing the scrolls of the Torah. Deeply impressed by the conviction that when the day is over the books of heaven will be sealed for another year, locking in the destiny of every soul until the next Day of Atonement, the participants cast themselves on God's compassion with a deep and almost desperate earnestness.

One Jewish tradition holds that it was on the tenth day of Tishri that Moses interceded for the Israelites following the golden calf debacle, pleading with God to forgive them even if it meant blotting his name out of (what is understood to be) the book of life—all in unconscious portrayal of the self-sacrificing Messiah to come (See Exodus 32:32).[4] In any case, the day does find its biblical genesis in the Israelites' wilderness wanderings, as outlined in Leviticus 16. It was the only day in the year when the high priest was permitted to step "inside the veil" into the most holy place of the tabernacle into the luminous presence of God, which hovered "in the cloud above the mercy seat" of the ark where the Ten Commandments were kept—and later the entire Torah (Leviticus 16:2; see Deuteronomy 31:26). Dressed in plain white linen, representing the humility and righteousness of Christ, he was to *"make atonement* for the Most Holy Place because of the uncleanness and rebellion of the Israelites, whatever their sins have been" (Leviticus 16:16 NIV, emphasis supplied).

Every other day of the year, penitents came confessing their sins over the innocent creatures whose shed blood, typifying the blood of Christ, was carried by the priests from the outer court to the holy place, or first apartment, of the tabernacle, signifying God's transference of sin from the sinner to the sanctuary—until the time when that sin would be blotted out. This blotting out was symbolically represented by the high priest's "once a year" forays into the most holy place, or second apartment, of the tabernacle, where the "accumulated" sin of the previous year was permanently dealt with in the presiding presence of God (Leviticus 16:34).[5] While the high priest entered in alone, he did so as the representative of God's people, who were to corporately join their hearts and minds to his by fasting, observing the day as a "sabbath of solemn rest," and afflicting their souls[6] with penitential sorrow—else they would be "cut off" and "destroy[ed]" from among God's people (Leviticus 16:31; 23:29, 30).

A divinely commissioned living parable, this elaborate sacrificial show-and-tell exemplifies the steps in the plan of salvation. First came the sacrifice whose blood was shed "once for all" to atone for "the sin of the world" (Hebrews 10:10; John 1:29). Then came Christ's ascension to "the [heavenly] tabernacle set up by the Lord, not by man," to mediate His atoning merits in behalf of the world, and especially the repentant sinner (Hebrews 8:2 NIV).[7] Last, in keeping with the pattern, comes the heavenly Day of Atonement, when our "great High Priest" will blot out the sin of all those who, throughout history, have united their hearts and minds with His by afflicting their souls in thorough repentance for sin (Hebrews 4:14).[8] All who have by faith received the reconciliation effected at the cross will indeed be reconciled with God and with each other for eternity. All who have refused this singular avenue of "at-one-ment" will have become "cut off" from God and will ultimately be "destroyed" from among His people.[9] At the conclusion of this cosmic Day of Atonement, the destiny of every soul is sealed for eternity—then Christ will return to claim His own.

CHECK IT OUT

This global, historically conclusive Day of Atonement equates, in effect, to a comprehensive pre-advent judicial review. And while it might be a foreign concept to most of the Christian world, it is solidly and amply grounded in Scripture, in the very character of God—and in logic itself. How could the "Son of Man ... come in his Father's glory with his angels" and "reward each person according to what he has done," if each person's character and actions, and the nature of their reward, have not first been decided (Matthew 16:27 NIV)? While God is not in the dark about such things, He lovingly condescends to make His ways understandable and accountable to His created, finite intelligences. For this reason, for the benefit of both fallen and unfallen, both human and angelic minds, He practices a two-phased method of doing judgment—first He investigates and makes available the facts, then He both executes and permits the appropriate outcome.[10] "Investigative judgment asks the question Has righteousness been done or not? ... Executive judgment, on the other hand, sets things right."[11] It's a judicial pattern God has followed with humanity since He established it at the inception of sin:

- When Adam and Eve recklessly plunged into disobedience, God first sought them out with searching questions, then partly permitted, partly executed their sentence (in which was also contained a promise for deliverance).
- When the post-Flood world again perversely arrayed itself against God, this time by confederating to build the infamous Tower of Babel, God first "came down to see the city and the tower which the sons of men had built," then subsequently executed the very creative solution of scattering them by confusing their language (Genesis 11:5).
- When "the outcry against Sodom and Gomorrah" came up before the Lord—who was already well aware of their perversity—He graciously said, "I will go down now and see whether they have done altogether according to the cry against it ... and if not, I will know" (Genesis 18:20, 21). Only after opening the case to angelic scrutiny and considering the intercessory input of Abraham, (from whom much of the "outcry" against the cities may have come), did God execute the deserved death penalty.

These constitute just a few examples of God's two-phased method of doing judgment. Yet so pervasive and entrenched is His "pattern of *investigating before He takes action*" that "one would have a hard time finding an example in the biblical record in which God executed judgment in a significant way before first taking that extra step of investigating."[12] For God, judgment is a very public, above-board matter. Throwing open the "record books" to the scrutiny of the intensely interested universe, He invites both angels and humans to "check it out" and judge for themselves whether His conclusions are just and reasonable. In fact, what this whole process of investigative review amounts to is not "God choosing who will be saved or lost, but rather *His recognizing those who have themselves chosen to be saved or lost.*" [13]

When the time comes, this latter principle will play out into some breathtakingly surprising scenarios, as many who have never been exposed to monotheism, let alone the name of Jesus, will be saved, while many who have considered themselves lifelong disciples will be lost. Paul said of the former:

> "When Gentiles [those who have not explicitly been exposed to the truth about God], who do not have the law, do by nature things required by the law, they are a law for themselves, even though they do not have the law, since they show that the requirements of the law are written on their hearts, their consciences also bearing witness, and their thoughts now accusing, now even defending them" (Romans 2:14, 15 NIV).

And Jesus said of the latter:

> "Not everyone who says to Me, 'Lord, Lord,' shall enter the kingdom of heaven, but he who does the will of My Father in heaven. Many will say to Me in that day, 'Lord, Lord, have we not prophesied in Your name, cast out demons in Your name, and done many wonders in Your name?' And then I will declare to them, 'I never knew you; depart from Me, you who practice lawlessness!'" (Matthew 25:21–23).

Indeed, "God does not show favoritism. … For it is not those who *hear* the law who are righteous in God's sight, but it is those who *obey* the law who will be declared righteous" (Romans 2:11, 13 NIV, emphasis supplied). It is a paradoxical truth of salvation that, while we are *saved* by grace through faith, we are *judged* by those behaviors that outwardly testify to our inward condition. Judgment is simply God placing His seal of acknowledgment upon that which we have implicitly and explicitly chosen, i.e., that which we have *become.*

The Wedding of the Lamb

While most of us would acknowledge that this is certainly the most fair and rational way to "do" judgment, if we're honest with ourselves, we also can't help but shudder at the thought of our sin-diseased selves being scrutinized by a sin-hating, holy God. How are we to reconcile God's need to judge and set things right in this sinful world—of which we are an integral part—with our need to somehow survive the crisis? As ever, the answer is found at the cross. As Jon Paulien has observed:

> "You could say that the final judgment went into session one Friday afternoon in Jerusalem. ... As God looked down on the human race in the person of Jesus, He saw in Him millenniums of unfaithfulness to the covenant. God then poured out on its representative, Jesus, the curse—the condemnation—that ... the whole human race deserved." [14]

As we've said, at the cross God achieved closure on the sin problem. If we accept as our own the judgment Christ experienced as our representative, [15] and daily surrender ourselves up to the purifying power of that reality, we need not face judgment a second time. There is no double jeopardy. While it's true that "we shall all stand before the judgment seat of Christ," if we have accepted as our own the death He experienced in our behalf, our life will at that time be "hidden with Christ in God" and we will "not come into judgment" (Romans 14:10; Colossians 3:3; John 5:24). When the Godhead and the watching universe gather to examine our case, they will see only our advocate, "Jesus Christ, the righteous" (1 John 2:1). Enthralled with His matchless charms, they will conclude that all who are truly identified with Him are safe to save—which is incredibly good news for otherwise lost sinners.

It's for this reason that the Bible also describes the preadvent judgment as a marriage—the permanent, inseparable melding of Christ and His beloved bride, the church. In the presence of innumerable witnesses, the heavenly bridegroom will become eternally wedded to all those who, since time began, have knit their hearts and minds with His. Like an eager Prince Charming, He will be carried by His ecstatic angelic friends to His Father to receive His betrothed, as envisioned by the prophet Daniel:

> "'I saw in the night visions, and, behold, one like the Son of man came with the clouds of heaven, and came to the Ancient of days, and they brought him near before him. And there was given him dominion, and glory, and a kingdom, that all people, nations, and languages, should serve him: his dominion is an everlasting dominion, which shall not pass away, and his kingdom that which shall not be destroyed" (Daniel 7:13, 14 KJV).

Jubilant with the realization that the wretched reign of sin will be forever ended and their beloved Jesus will be eternally joined to the love of His life, the whole host of heaven will shout the refrain, "Let us rejoice and be glad and give him glory! For the wedding of the Lamb has come, and his bride has made herself ready" (Revelation 19:7 NIV).

When Michael Stands Up

When will this marriage be finalized? That's up to the bride, as Christ would never force His affections on a "woman" who is not yet ready for such a mature commitment. So He waits with longing desire for her to "make herself ready." And while He waits, He works to bring it about. He works, through the Holy Spirit, to so inundate this world with truth that every inhabitant will be shaken out of complacency and into a confrontation with their sin and His righteousness.[16] He knows that this confrontation with reality will bring about a gradual polarization that will ultimately result in the "ripening" of a human harvest of either righteousness and eternal life, or condemnation and eternal death (Matthew 13:39–43).[17] When that point of no return has been reached, when every human being's fate has been sealed by their own informed choice, Christ will "*immediately*" conclude His work of reconciliation (Mark 4:29, emphasis supplied). Again, as Daniel envisioned:

> "At that time Michael[18] shall stand up, The great prince who stands watch over the sons of your people; And there shall be a time of trouble, Such as never was since there was a nation, Even to that time. And at that time your people shall be delivered, Every one who is found written in the book [of life]" (Daniel 12:1).

When Michael "stands up," He will make a pronouncement that is chilling in its finality, and infinitely sobering in its implications for every child of Adam:

> "He who is unjust, let him be unjust still; he who is filthy, let him be filthy still; he who is righteous, let him be righteous still; he who is holy, let him be holy still. And behold, I am coming quickly, and My reward is with Me, to give to every one according to his work" (Revelation 22:11, 12).

Until then, like a father pleading from his deathbed for his disaffected children to be reconciled, God pleads with

humanity from the cross of Christ to accept the reconciliation
He effected for us there (see 2 Corinthians 5:19, 20). The sin
that He has forgiven in Christ, He longs to eternally forget by
casting it "Into the depths of the sea" (Micah 7:19).

It's what this cosmic Day of Atonement is all about.

Endnotes

1. Adapted, with permission, from an article that appeared in 1996 in the *Jewish
    Bulletin of Northern California*, obtained from http://www.jewishsf.com/
    bk960920/layom.htm

2. Tishri, the first month of the Jewish year, falls during the Gregorian months
    of September and October.

3. Regarding this, one rabbi has commented, "God does not forgive those who
    smite their heart, but he pardons those whose heart smites them for the sins
    they committed." From "Yom Kippur Stories" at http://www.ou.org/chagim/
    yomkippur/ykstories.htm

4. Information obtained from "Yom Kippur: The Day of Atonement" found at
    http://www.amfi.org/kippur.htm and "Judaism 101" found at http://www.
    jewfaq.org/holiday4.htm

5. For a more complete explanation of the highly detailed Day of Atonement
    service, including the parts played by the "Lord's goat" (symbolizing Christ)
    and the "scapegoat"(symbolizing Satan), see Leviticus 16.

6. See Leviticus 16:29, 31; 23:27, 32. The Hebrew for "afflict" is *anah*, which
    Strong's Concordance (entry 6031) translates variously as "to abase self,
    afflict (-ion, self) ... chasten self, deal hardly with ... humble (self), hurt,
    ravish ... submit self, weaken."

7. This heavenly sanctuary, temple, or throne room was seen in vision by the
    apostle John, as noted in Revelation 7:15, and throughout chapters 11, 14, 15
    and 16.

8. As expressed in Acts 3:19–21, KJV: "Repent ye therefore, and be converted, that
    your sins may be *blotted out*, [i.e., obliterated] when the times of refreshing
    shall come from the presence of the Lord; And he shall send Jesus Christ,
    which before was preached unto you: Whom the heaven must receive until
    the times of restitution of all things."

9. The words "cut off" and "destroy," from Leviticus 23:29, 30, are, according to Strong's Concordance, translated respectively from the Hebrew *karath*, which means "to destroy or consume ... perish utterly," and *'abad*, which means "to wander away, i.e. lose oneself; by implication to perish ... have no way to flee."

10. While the pre-advent judicial review is for the direct benefit of the angels and the unfallen universe, the "millennial investigative judgment," which will be covered in chapter seventeen, will be tailored to answering the questions of the redeemed. Those who have not accepted salvation will understand the nature of their rejection in the context of the executive judgment, which will be addressed in chapter eighteen.

11. Jon Paulien, *Meet God Again for the First Time* (Hagerstown, MD: Review and Herald Publishing Association, 2003), pp. 95, 96.

12. John T. Anderson, *Investigating the Judgment: Divine Patterns of Judgment* (Hagerstown, MD: Review and Herald Publishing Association, 2003), pp. 104, 105, emphasis in original.

13. *Ibid.*, p. 24, emphasis supplied.

14. Paulien, p. 108.

15. While those familiar with the biblical narrative would experience this explicitly, those who have never heard but who respond intuitively to the Spirit's leading would experience it implicitly.

16. See Matthew 24:14; John 16:8–11.

17. As Marvin Moore insightfully notes in his book, *How to Think About the End Time*, "The close of probation will actually be a *process* that happens over a rather significant period of time" and "will not end for everyone at the same time." (Nampa, ID: Pacific Press Publishing Association, 2001), pp. 150, 151, emphasis supplied.

18. See chapter three, endnote 6, for the identity and the significance of the name Michael.

Chapter Fifteen

Holy Hero

"Who seeks a pusillanimous god, a god with a shriveled spirit? Who would worship a god who could look out at the world's callous brutality and simply say, 'Oh well. Boys will be boys.' The police are killing six-year-old children for money in the streets of Rio de Janeiro. Ten-year-old girls are being sold into prostitution in Bangkok. 'Oh well'? Who wants a God like that?"
—Mark Buchanan, *The Holy Wild* [1]

Few people know that the African Congo was, between 1890 and 1910, one of the major killing fields of modern times. Death toll estimates of between 5 and 8 million put it on a scale with Hitler's holocaust. The tyrant behind the tyranny was King Leopold of Belgium, a man who padded his own opulent existence by raping the Congo of ivory and rubber, gathered by the enslaved hands of its own people. Speaking of hands, Leopold's soldiers were required to account for each bullet used by sending a pair of human hands back to Belgium; they had to be smoke-dried first in order to be preserved. When the soldiers squandered their bullets on lion and elephant hunting anyway, they would simply account for the wasted cartridges by severing hands from living people. [2]

If the six o'clock news has left us with even a shred of sensitivity to these accounts of man's inhumanity to man, our reaction to King Leopold's crime is a nauseating mingling of disgust and anger. And this is as it should be. God through His Spirit has planted in our hearts a certain holy choler, ready to burst forth when we see the strong exploit the weak. And we have plenty of opportunities to express it—the oppression and abuse of the small people of the world is a phenomenon that has shamed human history as nothing else. In the face of atrocity, even the word "humane" becomes inaccurate, for what often defines humanity is the opposite of "humane" behavior.

Often, religion factors heavily into the inhumanity picture. The person of faith can be on either side of the abuse of power—the abused or, at times, the abuser. Even some forms of the Christian religion have been guilty of culturing oppressive and exploitive practices, leading to Christians persecuting Christians. This was the case in the persecution of the Dark Ages. In it, the followers of Christ were tortured and put to death, not in retaliation for evil, but for their refusal to obey the mandates of the church rather than the Word of God. *Fox's Book of Martyrs* is saturated with accounts of Christians who were skewered, strung up, roasted, ripped open and otherwise tortured and put to death for their faith—by others claiming to be Christians. Close to 400 pages amble interminably through gorily detailed accounts like this one:

> "They hanged both men and women by their hair or their feet, and smoked them with hay until they were nearly dead; and if they still refused to sign a recantation, they hung them up again and repeated their barbarities, until, wearied out with torments without death, they forced many to yield to them. Others they plucked off all the hair of their heads and beards with pincers. Others they threw on great fires, and pulled them out again, repeating it until they extorted a promise to recant. Some they stripped naked, and after offering them the most infamous

insults, they stuck them with pins from head to foot, and lanced them with penknives; and sometimes with red-hot pincers they dragged them by the nose until they promised to turn. Sometimes they tied fathers and husbands, while they ravished their wives and daughters before their eyes."[3]

Thousands more accounts that escaped Fox's notice have peeled off heaven's presses, known only by angels and God because they occurred in the obscure and unsung corners of the earth.

The Revelation of John records the sentiments of such martyrs. As the blood of Abel cried out to God, so the deaths of these believers are noted by God: "And they cried out with a loud voice, saying, 'How long, O Lord, holy and true, wilt Thou refrain from judging and avenging our blood on those who dwell on the earth?'" (Revelation 6:10). Our feeling is the same when we see horrendous abuse of power—how long will God wait? Why doesn't He do something? But martyrdom has its purpose. As the church father Tertullian said, "We multiply whenever we are mown down by you. The blood of Christians is seed."[4] Persecution is Satan's backfiring gun, actually growing the church he tries to snuff out. Witnessing faith that does not waver in the face of death has often led to devil-vexing mass conversion.

God takes the "How long?" question very seriously, giving a definitive answer: "Until the number of their fellow servants and their brethren who were to be killed even as they had been, should be completed also" (Revelation 6:10, 11). God will refrain from avenging the blood of the martyrs until "the number" of them is "completed"—in other words, when all the martyrs who ever will be slain have been slain. When will martyrdom end? When there is no more purpose for it, when no more conversions will take place because of it. That time will come when human probation ends, when every decision is unchangeably made for or against God, a time discussed in the last chapter. The unjust, the filthy, will be sealed in their lawless debasement. The righteous, the holy, will be fastened forever to their just and merciful Lord. Heretofore, God has restrained His anger toward human cruelty in order to extend His offer of salvation to wrongdoers. Wanting "all to come to repentance" (2 Peter 3:9), God has denied Himself the righteous impulse to rectify even horrific wrongs. When probation closes upon the human race, however, the God who has refrained from avenging the blood of the martyrs and other innocent sufferers can do so. And He can freely express His heartfelt rage at acts like those of King Leopold and his kind without destroying anyone who might otherwise be saved.

The apostles and prophets refer to this time as the "day of wrath," the "day of the Lord," the "wrath to come" and other similar expressions. Both the Old and New Testaments are liberally peppered with references to this time of unrestrained retribution.[5] The Revelation of John pinpoints where on the timeline of earth's history this "day of wrath" comes, as well as the events surrounding it.

First, the Message

The great catalyst of end-time events is found in Revelation 14:6–13. Like a bellows blowing upon sleeping coals, the message of the three angels enlivens the already existing elements of the conflict between good and evil. The angels, symbolizing the human agencies bearing the message of God, warn the earth of the coming cataclysm. In a "loud voice," the first angel proclaims that "the hour of His judgment is come" (v. 7) and enjoins worship of the Creator. The second pronounces the utterly fallen condition of the system of false religions, dubbed "Babylon the great, she who made all the nations drink of the wine ... of her immorality" (Revelation 14:8). The third angel's message

weighs in the heaviest of all, a siren-wail against the worship
of the infamous beast and its image:

> "If anyone worships the beast and his image, and
> receives a mark on his forehead or upon his hand, he
> also will drink of the wine of the wrath of God, which
> is mixed in full strength in the cup of His anger; and
> he will be tormented with fire and brimstone in the
> presence of the holy angels and in the presence of the
> Lamb" (vs. 9, 10).

What could move a loving Lamb to such extremes of
anger? He willingly endured crucifixion at the hands of the
very creatures He was sent to save. What has triggered this
expression of fury? As is often the case, God will tolerate
abuse to Himself, but when that same foul stream of animus
is discharged upon His children, God finally takes action.
Millennia of mercy have been snubbed, oceans of grace have
been polluted, and now the brute is turning to rend the little
ones. God is excruciatingly patient and infinitely kind, but
He is not without boundaries.

When the persecution of the ages reaches its zenith in
the end-time persecution, God at long last takes His stand
against flagrant evil. In the beast monster, God sees the
collective guilt of every oppressor, tyrant and despot that has
ever spoiled the earth. Identified as the little horn in Daniel's
prophecy, it will "wear down the saints of the Highest One,
and he will intend to make alterations in times and in law"
(Daniel 7:25). This audacious one will not only demand the
worship that belongs to God alone, but will dare to alter
His holy law. That law specifies how human beings should
relate to their Creator as well as their fellow creatures. The
first four commandments address who, how and when we
should worship. The last six commandments address how
we should relate to other human beings. Since the great
apostate attempts to usurp the worship that belongs to

God alone, he will tamper with the "laws" that deal with the worship of God. He "opposes and exalts himself above every so-called god or object of worship, so that he takes his seat in the temple of God, displaying himself as being God" (2 Thessalonians 2:4).

But the great usurper does not stop with altering the law of God. Reaching this height of arrogance, he works to enforce his own system of false religion. In a move to achieve world dominion, an edict is passed, stating that, "no one should be able to buy or sell, except the one who has the mark" (Revelation 13:17). Upon penalty of death (v. 15) the Lamb's followers refuse to take this mark, receiving instead the "seal of God" (9:4; 7:3), which is "the name of [God] written on their foreheads" (14:1). Ripened in the sun of Christ's righteousness, and in the latter rain of God's Spirit, the sealed believers "follow the Lamb wherever He goes" (14:4). An utterly polarized human race then witnesses "a time of trouble, Such as never was" (Daniel 12:1 NKJV).

ALL HELL BREAKS LOOSE ...

Of the time of trouble it can literally be said that all hell breaks loose. Christ has withdrawn from His position as mediator in the sanctuary above. God's Spirit has retreated from those who have received the mark of the beast. Evil, heretofore held in check by the divine agencies, is cut loose like a rabid dog. Those involved in the religious rites of beast-worship think themselves God's chosen people, yet their inspiration is straight from hell. They conspire to remove from the face of the earth the one blot of nonconformity, their thorn in the flesh, "who keep the commandments of God and their faith in Jesus" (Revelation 14:12). A death decree goes forth. The followers of the Lamb seem doomed again.

... All Heaven Breaks Loose

But this time the believer's blood would not sow faith, for the ground of the human race is hardened beyond the possibility of change. Sinners have, by their own choice, wedded themselves so fully to their sin that the two can never be separated. When in the "day of wrath" God finally reacts to the compiled sin of the ages, that sin is inextricably attached to sinners. They have been direct channels for evil as all hell has broken loose. In response, all heaven breaks loose. The "day of God" is God's day in the sense that He finally responds to sin as His holy and just nature fully dictates. For some 6,000 years, sin has been allowed to develop its true character to the tune of an often-silent heaven. Satan has had his day in the sun.[6] Finally, the true sentiments of a compassionate and brave Father come bursting forth. The blood of the innocent slain, the sweat of the slave, the tears of the oppressed, have soaked into the earth seemingly unnoticed. But in spite of appearances to the contrary, God has noticed. Now He responds as the divine hero to planet earth's evil bullies. God has for ages shown His love to the wicked by offering them mercy. Now He evinces His love to the wicked's victims by giving the wicked justice. He pours upon their heads the plagues of malignant sores, blood, fire and drought that they have earned.

"And I heard the angel of the waters saying, 'Righteous art Thou, who art and who wast, Oh Holy One, because Thou didst judge these things; for they poured out the blood of saints and prophets, and Thou hast given them blood to drink. They deserve it' " (Revelation 16:5, 6). Their punishment determined by their own crime, these vessels of evil finally feel something of what they made others feel.

THE DAY OF WRATH, THE DAY OF GOD

If the day of wrath is characterized by anything, it is an interpositional activity on God's part. The Revelation's portrait of God does not coincide well with modernity's New Age-hued designer God image. The former depicts a divine person judicially intervening in the affairs of men, the latter a warm, fuzzy force that will not sully itself with the task of retributive justice. Yet the prophetic pen throughout the Word is clear that the day of wrath entails divine action of an assertive, direct sort:

- "It will come as destruction from the Almighty" (Isaiah 13:6).
- "To make the land a desolation; and He will exterminate its sinners" (Isaiah 13:9).
- "Your dealings will return upon your own head" (Obadiah 1:15).
- "He will make a complete end, Indeed a terrifying one, Of all the inhabitants of the earth" (Zephaniah 1:18).
- "He will shatter kings in the day of His wrath" (Psalm 110:5).
- I will "destroy those who destroy the earth" (Revelation 11:18).

The pen of the apostle Paul harmonizes with that of the prophets as he speaks of the "day of wrath and revelation of the righteous judgment of God, who will render to every man according to his deeds" (Romans 2:5, 6). "Revelation" is from the Greek *Apokalupsis,* which means "disclosure." God's righteous judgment has, until the day of wrath, been undisclosed—held back by a mighty and merciful hand. But in the final assize, a heavenly changing of the guard takes place. Mercy, finally and fully beaten back, retreats. Justice marches in. God's character of love remains unflinchingly firm, but when mercy is fully insulted, that same hand that offered it for thousands of years brings forth a time of justice in all its formidable strength.

IS GOD KIDDING?

These passages sound so harsh. Is this really the same God as the meek and lowly Jesus who allowed Himself to be tortured and put to death without so much as a word of retaliation? Yes, it is Jesus Christ to whom judgment is committed, and through whom God will judge the world (John 5:22; Romans 2:16), yet He is acting in a different capacity than when He came to give up His life. And it is because He gave up His life in such utter selflessness that He can now judge with such boldness. He Himself knows, by agonizing experience, that every sacrifice was made to save the lost. He Himself felt the waves of pleading mercy meet ice-cold resistance again and again. Frustrated and heartbroken that the lost will not turn, and furious at their malicious acts toward the innocent, the One who was mighty to save sinners now becomes mighty to save the universe *from* sinners who will never change.

The intensity of these judgments is difficult for our "civilized" sensibilities to bear. Perhaps in these vivid accounts of judgment, we find a case of God merely laying claim to something He allows. Did He not do so in the case of Job?[7] Yes, but included in the story of Job is clear disclosure on the supernatural machinations behind Job's suffering. In Job's case, God allowed what Satan did, and we see plainly that this was the case. Can we then assume that in the passages that speak of divine wrath, God is merely laying claim, by virtue of His sovereignty, to something He allows the forces of evil to accomplish? We have no right to do so if God does not explicitly state it. To assume that God doesn't mean what He says is to make Him seem evasive or even dishonest.

Is God speaking figuratively? Yes, at times metaphoric expressions are used, but even metaphors indicate the form and function of what they symbolize. When the Bible speaks of the wrath of God being "poured out" from "golden bowls,"[8] it might be using figurative language (but then, it might not!), but those figures reveal that something that had previously been contained *in* heaven is now being released *from* heaven upon the earth.

There's no way around it. Divine retributive justice is a reality to which anyone who has confidence in the Word of God must ultimately bow. Oh, but how this biblical doctrine flies in the face of the rampant New Age teaching that makes God into a pervasive essence rather than the sovereign person that He is! New Age spirituality teaches the soul's own judgment of self, as if the human heart was capable, unaided, of self-management. It carefully preserves human pride by making each the judge of the subjective universe of his own creating. It positivizes God, neutering Him of justice, and turning His mercy into a license for sin.

The result is light years from the global harmony spiritualism purports to advance. It makes each person a deity and a law unto himself, free to trample upon the rights and comforts of others, all the while claiming his own righteousness. Only when human eyes see the reality of an absolute standard of judgment, mediated by an absolutely righteous and holy judge, can they begin to see their sin in the context of divine law. Spiritualism's version of judgment utterly fails to address the sin problem in such a comprehensive way. As God speaks forcefully and forthrightly of the punishment to befall the wicked, our eyes, so often glazed over by the world's sugar-coating, can see the seriousness of sin.

Viewed through the lens of the Holy Spirit, the doctrine of the judgment crystallizes and expands our concept of divine love. Author Mark Buchanan recalls the first time he was sure of his father's love. He and his brothers were playing street hockey when Mark was attacked by a bully three years his senior. He recalls falling under the blows, when suddenly they stopped:

"I looked up and saw my oppressor hovering against the sky, but now his face was terror-stricken. My father, who had been watching the bully's antics from our window, had come to my defense. He grabbed the boy by his coat collar and lifted him straight off the ground, like a man hanging from a noose, and shook him.

"'Don't you *ever*,' my father bellowed, 'hurt my son again!'

"It was enough. Here was a love I could count on to protect me, to defeat my enemies, to make things right. I basked in that for weeks. His wrath had made my father heroic in my eyes. I could sing in the shadow of his wings.

"Strange, but true. I learned to rest in my father's love because of his wrath."[9]

Endnotes

1. Mark Buchanan, *The Holy Wild* (Sisters, Oregon: Multnomah Publishers, 2003), p. 100.

2. Adam Hochschild, *King Leopold's Ghost* (Boston, New York: Houghton Mifflin Company, 1998), pp. 164, 165.

3. *Fox's Book of Martyrs*, edited by William Byron Forbush (Grand Rapids, MI: Zondervan Publishing House, 1967), p. 54.

4. This is a well-known statement which was found quoted at http://www.u-turn.net/6-1/seed.shtml

5. "Day of the Lord," see Isaiah 13:6, 9, 13; Jeremiah 23:20; 30:24, Lamentations 2:22; Ezekiel 7:19; 13:5; 30:3; Joel 1:15; 2:1, 11, 31; 3:14, Amos 5:18–20; Obadiah 1:15; Zephaniah 1:7, 8, 14, 18; 2:2, 3; Malachi 4:5; Acts 2:20; 1 Corinthians 5:5; 1 Thessalonians 5:2; 2 Thessalonians 2:2; 2 Peter 3:10; "Day of God," see Romans 2:5; 2 Peter 3:12; Revelation 16:14; "Day of Wrath," see Psalm 110:5; Proverbs 11:4; Zephaniah 1:15;

Revelation 6:17; "Wrath of the Lamb," see Revelation 6:16; 14:10; "Wrath to Come," see Matthew 3:7; Luke 3:7; 1 Thessalonians 1:10; "Day of Fury," "Anger" or "Indignation," see Job 21:30; Isaiah 13: 9, 13; Job 20:28; Lamentations 1:12; 2:1, 21, 22; Zephaniah 2:2, 3; Ezekiel 22:24.

6. With occasional interventions from God, which in and of themselves were evidence of a time of full intervention, see 2 Peter 2:4–6; Jude 5–7.

7. See Job 2:3, and Chapter Eight of this book.

8. Revelation 15:7.

9. Mark Buchanan, *The Holy Wild* (Sisters, Oregon: Multnomah Publishers, 2003), pp. 101, 102.

Chapter Sixteen

Power to the People

"The risen saints' assessments of the divine judgments will place the wisdom, justice, and goodness of both the Father and the Son forever beyond question."
—Hans K. LaRondelle, *Light for the Last Days* [1]

"The modern embarrassment with God's wrath is unknown to Scripture."
—Tim Crosby, "Does God Get Angry?" [2]

*T*he Lord of the Flies by William Golding was, for many years, standard reading fare for junior-high youth. Perhaps this was no accident. Perhaps the educational establishment wanted to infuse the sometimes-savage world of public high school with a message of the limitations of jungle power.

The plot finds a group of schoolboys marooned on an island when their plane is shot down. While they begin their fight for survival in solidarity, they eventually faction off under the diplomatic and fair Ralph, the originally appointed chief of the group, and the aggressive and violent Jack—who succeeds in seducing the majority, leaving Ralph with just a few. The larger pack descends into savagery, using a wild pig's head as a cult symbol and a frenzied dance as a religious rite. Killings begin. First it's just wild pigs, but then a gentle boy named Simon is riddled with spears when the group assumes he is an enemy. Finally, Piggy, the story's symbol of equity and justice, is purposely crushed under a boulder. The end of the story finds Ralph alone and running, then crawling, for his life. As his sun-browned and dirty body hauls itself over the beach, his would-be murderers on his heels, he is suddenly halted by a gleaming white-uniformed naval officer. Jack and the pack are stopped in their tracks. In the presence of greater authority, the little man-hunters are reduced again to powerless children.

The officer asks, "Who's boss here?"

"I am," Ralph says loudly.[3]

The reader is left with the reality that the boys would be going home—to family, to baths, to food, but also to the courts of justice where Ralph himself, so recently hunted by them, would have a part in judging them guilty.

The plot is classic—a disenfranchised good guy suffers under the arrogant domination of a powerful enemy. The bad guy's antipathy heightens into a thirst for blood. The situation is taken to the nail-biting edge, when suddenly an unexpected miracle takes place, vindicating the oppressed and bringing the enemy's sword down upon his own head. We might call it a radical shift in power, a reversal.

The final hours of earth's history will witness a similar power shift. During the time of trouble, God's people are judged by the great powers of the earth to be the vilest of criminals. Things come down to the wire when a death decree is passed, putting the 144,000[4] protagonists in harm's way. Suddenly, a divinely interruptive sweep of events brings the world's great powers to nothing, and places the power in the hands of the persecuted.

ON A WHITE HORSE

When the last of the seven bowls of wrath are poured out upon earth, a voice is heard from the temple in heaven, shouting, "It is done!" Supernatural forces work through natural elements to create a scene of complete chaos. Lightning scorches the earth as deafening thunder pounds the air. An earthquake that defies the Richter scale rends the terrain into shards. Hundred-pound hailstones pummel the ground, crushing flesh and bone, urging forth the dying blasphemies of lost souls. Nature heaves under the weight of the plagues, and humankind finds itself ridden with disease and unrest of every kind. Evil forces that God has released, as well as good forces that He has enlisted, make for scenes of devastation everywhere.[5] It's not called a "time of trouble *such as never was*" for nothing.[6]

And then, to the wreckage, Jesus comes in glory.

"And I saw heaven opened; and behold, a white horse, and He who sat upon it is called Faithful and True; and in righteousness He judges and wages war" (Revelation 19:11). In full regalia, with incandescent eyes and a jewel-encrusted crown, His lush robes and glittering shield embellished with the insignia "King of Kings, and Lord of Lords," Jesus rides to the rescue of His waiting children. Escorted by an angel entourage numbering in the tens of thousands,[7] He who was once a carpenter comes back as the venerable king of the cosmos. But a strange phenomenon takes place as the believers revel in the presence of love; the wicked multitudes react to the same spectacle as to a raging, devouring inferno, crying, "Fall on us and hide us from the presence of Him who sits on the throne, and from the wrath of the Lamb; for the great day of their wrath has come; and who is able to stand?" (Revelation 6:16, 17). The light of love's countenance burns the fog from their memories, and they suddenly recall the many times His sweet voice begged them to turn to Him. Peeling back the layers of denial, these unwelcome memories trigger an anxiety so deep that they dive beneath rocks in the hopes of silencing them. They are sorry, oh, so sorry, but it is not true remorse for sin. In the face of incalculable loss, the rebels against God experience a Judas-like guilt that laments the personal consequences of sin absent from a sorrow for the sin itself.

SOME RAISED, SOME CHANGED

The return of the life-giver unearths more than memories—it brings forth lives that have been long locked in the grave. As Jesus promised Caiaphas, those who played a prominent role in His crucifixion will be called forth to witness His second advent.[8] Christ brings to life again those figures of human history in whom sin had developed to its hideous height, that they might stand with their modern counterparts, the bedeviled followers of the beast power. Together these epitomes of evil will witness the searing glory of the coming of the Lord.

"Behold, He is coming with the clouds, and every eye will see Him, even those who pierced Him; and all the tribes of the earth will mourn over Him" (Revelation 1:7). The sight is too much. Raised in mortal bodies, the wicked ones cannot withstand the brightness of His glory any more than their sinful hearts can withstand the light of His love. The most wicked of all time Christ will "slay with the breath of His mouth and bring to an end by the appearance of His coming" (2 Thessalonians 2:8). And even this is borne of love. "God's hatred of evil is just as strong as His love of good. His holiness is benign toward right and malevolent toward sin, just as a fire may comfort or destroy. His glory is toxic to evil, just as oxygen, which is life giving to humans, is toxic to certain types of bacteria. God is matter, and sin is anti-matter, and whenever matter encounters anti-matter there is a holocaust."[9]

But Jesus' mission is more than the judgment of the cruel of the earth. Judgment always has a compassionate aspect, for justice to an oppressor means final deliverance for the oppressed. As the judge-deliverer, Jesus comes to the rescue of those cruelly treated, those who have been locked in the prison house of the grave by Satan himself. In obedience to His voice, the earth uncovers the great multitudes of God's faithful through the ages. While the evil conspirators bear the gray shadow of death, the righteous are raised without a trace of mortality, radiant with eternal health, "imperishable."[10]

After the sleeping saints rise, the living saints, so recently haggard with fear and hunted by their oppressors, are changed into a glorified form that shields them forever from the encroachments of death. "Then we who are alive and remain shall be caught up together with them in the clouds to meet the Lord in the air, and thus we shall always be with the Lord" (1 Thessalonians 4:17). The great heavenly reunion begins, with separated loved ones falling into each other's arms, children finding their once-bereaved parents, and friends looking with pleasure upon the ageless faces of those with whom they once grew old. Together with the great masses of the saved, they are escorted into the intimate presence of God, to stand on the "sea of glass mixed with fire," and to sing "the song of Moses … and the song of the Lamb" (Revelation 15:2, 3).

The earth is desolate. The charred bodies of those who could not withstand the brightness of Christ's coming are strewn over its surface. Only Satan and his devils live on to witness the havoc they have wreaked. As the "scapegoat" symbolically bore the punishment for Israel's sins into the wilderness at the close of the Day of Atonement,[11] so Satan will ultimately bear the punishment for the sins he has caused humanity to commit into the "wilderness" of a desolate planet. Without a soul to torment or tempt, he is, in the truest sense, "bound ... for a thousand years ... that he should not deceive the nations any longer, until the thousand years [are] completed" (Revelation 20:2, 3). Without any of his standard escape mechanisms, he is forced to reflect upon his crimes against man and God and his grim future before the highest court in the universe.

THE THOUSAND-YEAR INVESTIGATION

Many thousands of miles away, in a blissfully busy heaven, the redeemed have a monumental task before them. The vision of John revealed "thrones, and they sat upon them, and judgment was given to them" (Revelation 20:4). Saints judging in heaven? Yes. Years before John's vision, Paul had appealed to his congregation in Corinth to refrain from lawsuits against one another on the basis that "the saints will judge the world" and "angels" (1 Corinthians 6:2, 3). And this is as it should be. While our present, partial knowledge renders us incapable of judging others, at this time "the Lord ... will both bring to light the things hidden in the darkness and disclose the motives of men's hearts" (1 Corinthians 4:5). This greater insight comes through the examination of the books of heaven, spoken of by the prophet Isaiah: "Behold, *it is written* before Me, I will not keep silent, but I will repay ... Both their own iniquities and the iniquities of their fathers together" (Isaiah 65:6, 7, italics supplied). Malachi also speaks of a record of right-doing: "Then those who feared the Lord spoke to one another, and the Lord gave attention and heard it, and a book of remembrance was written before Him for those who fear the Lord and who esteem His name" (Malachi 3:16).

With full disclosure of every thought and motive open to them, the redeemed partner with God Himself in probing the cases of the lost. While God is fully capable of unilaterally judging the wicked, His more democratic approach to the judgment process encourages the trust and openness that make heaven the perfectly safe place that it is. No doubt many will inquire as to why certain ones are not present in the heavenly abode. In answer to their searching questions, the "hidden things" will be brought to view, exposing the underbelly of many lives that seemed above reproach. For a thousand years, the saints' questions about the lost are answered, one falling tear at a time. Equipped with divine documentation that penetrates beyond the scope of human vision, they realize that each and every soul's destination was fixed by its own choice. As Dietrich Bonhoeffer said of church discipline—and his statement applies to judgment in all its forms—"Excommunication is really nothing more than the recognition of a state of affairs that already exists, for the unrepentant sinner has condemned himself already."[12]

Heart by heart the redeemed surrender to the fact that the lost would only loathe a selfless, holy heaven. Mind by mind they realize that those who are not present have, of their own choice, clung fatally to sin, which was doomed to banishment from the universe. There is a settling in, an acceptance, a sigh of "so be it." Finally, the decision of the heavenly court is reached unanimously by a jury of peers. Not one doubt as to whether justice was done will mar eternity.

No true closure could come to the sin problem without this final review of, and careful dealing with, each and every lost person's case. Embedded in God's very nature is the drive to consume the darkness. Only through this carefully monitored exposing of humankind's criminal record can sin be seen for what it is, and thus be swallowed up in the light that will grace eternity.

Imagine if God were to skip this crucial step. Imagine if He were to excuse Satan himself, dismissing the problem like a bad headache, hoping it would just go away. What if He left every rape and murder unaddressed, forgot every widow-making war conceived in power-lust, and ignored every man-made disease that turned life into a torture chamber?

How would we feel if God shrugged at every scene of needless poverty induced by the excesses of the rich? Could we love a God who excused, through inaction, the great conspiracy of evil that has made life a futility for millions, and swept many of them into a hopeless eternity? Could there be any true peace in the hereafter, any real trust between God and His children, if those evils were never scrupulously exposed? None. Only a certain callused keeping of the order that characterizes a dysfunctional family who maintains a code of silence and a refuge of denial.

God never asks us to regard evil with indifference, only to wait patiently for the Lord to take matters into His own hands: "Never take your own revenge, beloved, but leave room for the wrath of God, for it is written, 'Vengeance is Mine, I will repay' says the Lord" (Romans 12:19). C.S. Lewis writes of human vengeance, "Revenge loses sight of the end in the means, but its end is not wholly bad—it wants the evil of the bad man to be to him what it is to everyone else."[13] Any heart in whom the Spirit of God has an audience will feel a divinely infused desire to see the wrong acknowledged, and even felt, by the wrongdoer. We will be unsettled by evil, and even more unsettled by God's seeming indifference to it. But while God's inaction might bring a certain longing for justice, it is our calling to believe that He does care, and will act, and to let that reality keep us from becoming self-appointed cosmic cops and ego-crazed vigilantes. Our desire for justice is God-implanted, our carnal method of bringing it about is not. The task of a disciple is to submit to the discipline of waiting for God to intervene, all the while hoping for the preferred form of justice, which is repentance, in which the penalty for wrong is fulfilled in Jesus Christ. Even then, there will be a recognition of wrong done, and true confession, which brings relief to the heart of the sufferer. Life gives God's children plenty of practice in this discipline of foregoing justice. In the face of nearly universal evil, they wait for a time when "God Himself is judge" (Psalm 50:6). But the divine irony is this: After so many years of subordinating their desire for justice to the will of God, to His timing and infinite wisdom, God's followers are given a partnership in the judicial process. Significantly, this process comes at a time when punishment can no longer deter the wrongdoer, for probation is closed. Then punishment comes simply because it is deserved. And even this is a necessary expression of God's character of love. Lewis explained it this way:

> "Some enlightened people would like to banish all conceptions of retribution or desert from their theory of punishment and place its value wholly in the deterrence of others or the reform of the criminal himself. They do not see that by so doing they render all punishment unjust. What can be more immoral than to inflict suffering on me for the sake of deterring others if I do not deserve it?" [14]

The discipline of enduring injustice on earth fits God's followers to deal fairly with it in heaven. God will trust His children to be impartial, because they have learned to surrender judgment to Him. Their enduring of unfair treatment that their enemies might receive the message of forgiving grace has qualified them to be compassionate, fair judges.

In God's order of things, self-giving always preempts judgment. God's children have lived with the salvation of sinners in focus. They have followed the Lamb wherever He goes in self-abandoning love for others (Revelation 14:4). Now He can trust them to judge with the good of the universe, the good of others, and even the good of those they judge, in full view.

Endnotes

1.   Hans K. LaRondelle, *Light for the Last Days* (Nampa, Idaho: Pacific Press Publishing,1999), p. 140.

2. Tim Crosby, "Does God Get Angry?" *Ministry,* July, 1990.

3. William Golding, *Lord of the Flies* (New York: The Berkley Publishing Group, 1954), p. 186.

4. See Revelation 7:4. Whether this is a literal number or not is arguable.

5. Revelation 16:17–21.

6. Daniel 12:1, KJV.

7. See Matthew 24:30, 31; 26:53. "Twelve legions" is 72,000.

8. See Matthew 26:64; Revelation 1:7.

9. Crosby, "Does God Get Angry?" *Ministry Magazine,* July, 1990.

10. See 1 Corinthians 15:52.

11. As per Leviticus 16.

12. Dietrich Bonhoeffer, *The Cost of Discipleship* (New York: Simon & Schuster, 1995), p. 291.

13. C.S. Lewis, *The Problem of Pain* (New York: Macmillan Publishing Company, 1962), p. 94.

14. *Ibid.*

Chapter Seventeen

God's Last Goodbye

" 'Whither is God?' he cried. 'I shall tell you. We have killed him—you and I. All of us are his murderers. ... How shall we, the murderers of all murderers, comfort ourselves? What was holiest and most powerful of all that the world has yet owned has bled to death under our knives. Who will wipe this blood off us? What water is there for us to clean ourselves? What festivals of atonement, what sacred games shall we have to invent? Is not the greatness of this deed too great for us? Must not we ourselves become gods simply to seem worthy of it?' "
—Friedrich Nietzsche, *Parable of the Madman* [1]

So raved the wild-eyed protagonist of German poet and philosopher Friedrich Nietzsche's *Parable of the Madman*. Part prophetic plaint and part atheistic boast, these and similar rants burned their way from Nietzsche's feverish, syphilitic mind to his prolific pen, inaugurating the modern age of nihilism. "God is dead," Nietzsche pugnaciously asserted, "and we have killed him." Having furiously "sow[n] the wind" of militant atheism and amorality, he scratched out the end of his life as a lonely lunatic, leaving us—his philosophical progeny—to "reap the whirlwind" of angst and alienation (Hosea 8:7).

"One of the great blind spots of a philosophy that attempts to disavow God," writes Ravi Zacharias, "is its unwillingness to look into the face of the monster it has begotten and own up to being its creator."[2] Yet paradoxically, the very One who has mercifully shielded His vilifiers from having to look full into the face of their carefully crafted Frankenstein is God Himself. But the day is coming when He will tear away the protective veil and allow these monster-makers to discern the deadly matrix of their creation in the undimmed light of His countenance.

MURDER, THEY WROTE

For a thousand years, since it "reel[ed] to and fro like a drunkard" at the cataclysmic second coming of Christ, the earth has lain a vast, blasted graveyard, sterile and still (Isaiah 24:20). Ragged ruins jut like broken teeth from its fractured surface. Splintered remnants of uprooted trees, long since petrified, protrude from between blackened boulders. Not a green thing trembles. Not a breathing thing stirs. Until, incredibly, living bodies begin to materialize among the craters and the ruins. Bodies almost without number, varied beyond description, from strapping, Herculean giants to spectral, hollow-eyed waifs ravaged by age and disease.[3] Far from being the opening scene for the latest ghostly chiller, this is the dawning of Judgment Day.[4] And these are the resurrected bodies of the damned.[5]

Why has God summoned these lost souls from sleep? Why not let them remain in oblivion—they're just going to die again anyway. Because the second, eternal death they'll soon face brings a necessary, divinely orchestrated closure to the great controversy between good and evil. It's the only viable conclusion to a cosmic conflict that has been all about freedom of choice, and taking responsibility for that freedom of choice, in the context of God's policy of full disclosure. And it's precipitated by a cosmic confrontation with reality—a dual encounter with the God they've spent a lifetime evading, and the secret self they've spent a lifetime concealing. To facilitate this confrontation, God permits the lost to act out the deepest, yet for the most part unconscious, desire of their hearts. He permits them to attempt His murder.

As they went into their graves, so they reappear, compelled by the same enmity toward Christ and the same spirit of rebellion that inspired them while they lived. Whether or not they were conscious of this enmity during their lives, it was the actuating principle that shaped their characters and determined their destinies. Incorrigible consciences and characters intact, they rise from their long sleep, determined to superimpose their sovereign wills upon their brave new world and upon each other.[6]

Instantly, Satan seizes the moment.[7] A millennium of morbidly reliving his monumental failure, with no one to torment but his god-forsaken cronies, has sharpened his appetite for dominance and revenge. Posturing, as ever, as "an angel of light," he exploits the disaffection of the lost and fastens their allegiance to himself (2 Corinthians 11:14). Having rejected Christ, the only source of truth, they are powerless to discern or resist his deceptions. Styling himself their redeemer and rightful king, he leads them captive across "the breadth of the earth" and with them "surround[s] the camp of the saints and the beloved city"—the New Jerusalem, which has descended from heaven in luminescent splendor (Revelation 20:9; see 21:2).

What can be the purpose of this insane endeavor but to wrest from His throne their Creator and Redeemer, and thrust in His place the antithesis of all He represents? In this outwardly beautiful but inwardly malevolent fallen angel, the lost see the incarnation of everything they have cherished— the irrepressible ego, the will to power, the refusal to bow to anyone or anything greater than oneself. As they look in the face of this monster of deception, they believe they see the Superman[8] who will deliver them from the bondage of moral absolutism and empower them to become gods of a universe of their own making. Yet at the root of this consensual deception, and all the denial and sophisticated rationalizations it has spawned, is the compulsion to murder the only One who can give them life and a character with which to value it.

It's time for God to tear away the veil.

CONFRONTATION WITH REALITY

Just as these misguided revolutionaries imagine their goal to be within their grasp, they are arrested by a scene of transcendent glory. Above the city appears "a great white throne" upon which sits the Son of God, whose radiance floods the fractured earth (Revelation 20:11). As His luminous eyes survey the murderous throng before Him, the light of truth breaks upon their darkened minds like a blinding sunburst. Naked before those eyes, every inner chamber of their character is exposed, and they see their every sin and defect carved upon their consciousness as if in letters of fire.

In stark contrast to this horrific revelation of self, they are confronted by the self-emptying character of Christ. At last, they see Him as He is, "a God so full of mercy that He becomes man and dies by torture to avert that final ruin from His creatures."[9] Eyes riveted to the benevolent face and the light streaming from the saving scars in His hands (see Habakkuk 3:4), they are gripped by the certainty that the Good Shepherd could do no more to win their love and secure their salvation. He has spent Himself utterly for their sakes. The wall of evasion and denial behind which they have hidden from His grace is reduced to rubble, as each is made to "understand the nature of his own rejection of truth."[10]

"Before the vision of Calvary with its mysterious Victim … every lying excuse [is] swept away."[11] Another chance,

198 A Deep but Dazzling Darkness

another lifetime, wouldn't change their destiny. They are not saved, not because God didn't exhaust all His resources to save them, but because they have perversely and irrationally rejected Him. Reflecting upon their recent murderous attempt, they see that, if it were possible, they would annihilate their source of life—indeed, by their life choices, they in essence already have. Having invalidated their "right" to live, they realize there is "no place for them" to continue (Revelation 20:11).[12]

The realization is too much. Gazing on the glorious city that they have unfit themselves to occupy, looking upon the God of love they will never truly comprehend, they fall prostrate and exclaim in an agony of despair and self-loathing, "Just and true are thy ways, O King of the ages … for thy judgments have been revealed" (Revelation 15:3, 4 RSV). The evidence has been presented; God's judgment has been revealed. The lost are excluded from eternal life at their own initiative, and they are constrained to agree with their just sentence of death.

Yet their dual admission of guilt and justice is not inspired by a sudden infatuation with truth. There is within their seared consciences no repentance for sin, no change of purpose, no hatred of evil. Their confession is forced from their guilty souls by an awful sense of condemnation and a "fearful expectation of judgment" (Hebrews 10:27). How so? Because it dawns on these unfortunates that, not only have they forfeited an eternity of bliss by rejecting the source of that bliss; not only will they suffer their sentence of death at their own perverse initiative—they also see with devastating clarity that they will experience all of this in the context of a terrifying confrontation with the undiluted justice of God.

They do not go gently into their eternal good night. Fastening their frenzied eyes on the angelic monster that has so masterfully deceived them, they now discern the defeated form of a malicious, petty tyrant, and exclaim in disbelief, "Is this the [one] who made the earth tremble, Iho shook kingdoms? Who made the world as a wilderness And destroyed its cities, Who did not open the house of his prisoners? Have you also become as weak as we? Have you become like us?" (Isaiah 14:16, 17, 10). The veil has been torn away. Hating their fallen "Superman" with a hot, visceral hatred, they turn on Satan and his agents-in-deception, and with the furious abandon of the condemned attempt to tear them to pieces. Absorbed in their efforts to annihilate him and each other, their end comes upon them suddenly, like a whirlwind. The Bible tersely describes this incendiary finale in these words, "Fire came down from God out of heaven and devoured them" (Revelation 20:9).

THREE DIMENSIONAL JUDGMENT

What can be known about this mysterious fire and its outcome, the "second death?"[13] What has God made plain to us about it? As theologian Clark Pinnock has noted, "Jesus' teaching about the eternal destiny of the wicked is bold in its warnings but modest when it comes to precise description."[14] Yet while Jesus didn't exploit our fears or indulge our taste for the sensational by dwelling on the details, He had plenty to say about final punishment. And He consistently referred to it, as C.S. Lewis has remarked, "under three symbols: first, that of *punishment* ... second, that of *destruction* .... and thirdly, that of privation, exclusion, or *banishment* into 'the darkness outside.'"[15] Let's examine these three symbolic representations by turn:

Punishment: Jesus said, "That servant *who knew his master's will,* and did not ... do according to his will, *shall be beaten with many stripes.* But he *who did not know,* yet committed things deserving of stripes, *shall be beaten with few.* For everyone to whom much is given, from him much will be required; and to whom much has been committed, of him they will ask the more" (Luke 12:47, 48, emphasis supplied).

What Jesus is enunciating here is the principle of *distributive* justice, the idea that there will be gradations of punishment based on degree of accountability. This accountability, or guilt, is what has been distilled from the millennial judgment, when the motives and actions of the lost were weighed against all the other variables of their lives, including hereditary and environmental factors, implicit and explicit knowledge of the truth, and truth that could have been known but was neglected.[16]

What exactly this fiery punishment consists of is impossible for us to fully understand, though it would seem to have both intrinsic and extrinsic implications. Surely, to stand in the presence of a righteous God while burdened with unresolved guilt would result in a psychological meltdown of such magnitude that death would seem a welcome release. Yet the Bible makes clear that there is also a distinctly extrinsic dimension to final punishment. While "God is love," and remains so in the final judgment, this love compels Him to be righteously angry with these unrepentant victimizers whose sin was not committed in a vacuum. It was as poisonous seed sown broadcast in the lives of others, bringing a toxic harvest of oppression, seduction, degeneracy and death, multiplied many times over. It is right for God to "render" to them the hot disapproval of His wrath "according to what [they have] done" (Romans 2:6 NIV). It is inevitable that God, who is a "consuming fire" to sin, must ultimately consume those who have become totally identified with sin by refusing to be parted from it (Hebrews 12:29).[17] And it is necessary for God to bring closure to the cognitive dissonance of the redeemed, who all their lives struggled to reconcile His hatred of sin with His apparent tolerance of it. Upon such closure the stability of the universe rests.

Banishment: While a searing collision with God's wrath and banishment to "outer darkness"[18] would seem to be

mutually exclusive experiences, Jesus has described the fate
of the lost in just these paradoxical terms. While they suffer
from a surfeit of hot confrontation, they are simultaneously
being sucked into a tidal wave of blackest despair. Shut
away from the joys and comforts that have made life sweet,
alienated from the warmth of human love and affection,
deprived of God's life-giving blessing and favor, these god-
forsaken souls experience in their every nerve and cell what it
means to be made "a curse" (Galatians 3:13). Having rejected
Christ's being made a curse for them, they must, by default,
bear within themselves the soul-destroying experiential
"knowledge" of becoming an abomination, an offscouring, a
thing utterly "despised" and "rejected" (Isaiah 53:11, 3).

All their lives they have been hostilely dependent upon
God's unmerited favor. Ever taking, ever rendering a stoic
thanklessness in return, they have bitten the hand that has fed
and saved them until it can no longer sustain them without
doing violence to their own freedom of choice. So it must
forever withdraw and leave them to themselves. As Lewis has
so poignantly observed, "In the long run the answer to all
those who object to the doctrine of hell, is itself a question:
'What are you asking God to do?' To wipe out their past
sins and, at all costs, to give them a fresh start, smoothing
every difficulty and offering every miraculous help? But He
has done so, on Calvary. To forgive them? They will not be
forgiven. *To leave them alone?* Alas, I am afraid that is what He
does."[19] Left alone in their imploding universe, the lost finally
slip into a featureless oblivion from which there is no return.

Destruction: It is enough. Justice is satisfied. As horrific
as this vision of final punishment is, thank God it's not
the version that is generally insisted upon in the name of
Christianity. Thankfully, the "Judge of all the earth" is not a
vindictive tyrant who blasts His enemies with "an unending
stream of anger that will pour forth continually from [His]
inner being ... for all eternity."[20] Such a loathsome depiction
of God is more worthy of the character of Satan, who is, in

fact, the instigator of this faith-destroying lie. When God's righteous wrath has fulfilled its just and merciful purpose, those who have identified with sin, and all of its death- and disease-producing fallout, will be "ashes under the soles of [the] feet" of the redeemed—and that figuratively, as the scorched earth is recreated into the paradise it was always meant to be (Malachi 4:3).

How could it be otherwise? God alone is immortal; we are inherently mortal (see 1 Timothy 6:16). "God gives us life and God takes it away. There is nothing in the nature of the human soul that requires it to live forever. The Bible teaches conditionalism: God created humans mortal with a capacity for life everlasting, but it is not their inherent possession. Immortality is a gift God offers us in the gospel, not an inalienable possession."[21] Gifts, no matter how vital, cannot be forced upon the object of the giver's affection. If the lost were forced to live in a heaven ruled by other-centered love, it would be to them an intolerable hell. Eternal nonexistence is their just and merciful portion.

ALL THINGS NEW

Is this the way God would have it? Not at all. He is "not willing that any should perish but that all should come to repentance" (2 Peter 3:9). Moment by moment His Spirit pleads with humanity, "Look to Me and be saved, All you ends of the earth," "For why should you die?" (Isaiah 45:22; Ezekiel 33:11). "By the grace of God," Christ has already satisfied the claims of justice and "taste[d] death for everyone," rendering the second death unnecessary (Hebrews 2:9). He has borne our guilt, absorbed the hot arrows of wrath that we deserve; for our sakes He has been cast into outer darkness as a thing despised and rejected. He has done, and continues to do, all in His power to avoid having to say this last, heartrending goodbye.

How can we respond to such a God? We can let His sin-consuming Holy Spirit purify and separate us from sin and self now, so we might spare Him the heartache of destroying us with His glory later. We can accept His all-sufficient sacrifice in our behalf, surrendering up the vain, self-sufficient works that can only condemn us in the judgment as rejectors of Christ. We can recognize that the darkness we've thought we have discerned in Him originates in the one who has lied to us about Him all our lives.

We can let Him daily make of us a new creation, so our hearts will beat in harmony with His in that day when He joyously sweeps His arms across His purified, recreated earth and exclaims, "Behold, I make all things new!" (Revelation 21:5).

Endnotes

1. From Friedrich Nietzsche's *Parable of the Madman,* as quoted in Ravi Zacharias, *Can Man Live Without God* (Nashville: Word Publishing Group, 1994), pp. 18, 19.

2. *Ibid.,* p. 22.

3. This is reflective of the degeneration the human race has experienced since the inception of sin.

4. In the larger sense, the "day of judgment" could also be said to have begun with the finalization of the pre-advent judgment, which judicially "separated" the "sheep from the goats;" this separation began to be acted upon with the dispensing of the plagues and in the events surrounding the second coming. As was noted in Chapter Fifteen, God first *investigates* the facts, then *executes* the judgment called for.

5. As per Revelation 20:5: "The rest of the dead"—those who had not been included in the first resurrection that took place at the second coming—"did not live again until the thousand years were finished."

6. The Bible clearly teaches that "the dead know nothing" (Ecclesiastes 9:5), that the interval between an individual's death and resurrection equates to an unconscious "sleep" (see Matthew 9:24; Mark 5:39; Luke 8:52; John 11:11–14), and that when God restores them to consciousness, He does so by reconstituting the neurological framework on which consciousness

is predicated: "It is not possible to separate individual neurons from their functions; if it were possible, then a thought could be freed from its neurological base, and the mind could be seen as something separate from the brain, a free-floating consciousness that could be considered a 'soul …'[But] science can demonstrate no way for the mind to occur except as a result of the neurological functioning of the brain. Without the brain's ability to process various types of input in highly sophisticated ways, the thoughts and feelings that constitute the mind would simply not exist." From Andrew Newberg, M.D., Eugene D'Aquili, Ph.D., and Vince Rause, *Why God Won't Go Away: Brain Science and the Biology of Belief* (New York: Ballantine Books, 2001), pp. 33, 34.

7. As noted in our last chapter, Satan is confined to the desolated earth during the millennium, "so that he should deceive the nations no more till the thousand years were finished. … But when the thousand years have expired, Satan will be released from his prison and will go out to deceive the nations which are in the four corners of the earth" (Revelation 20:3, 7, 8).

8. Nietzsche's godless, amoral model man, as idealized in *Thus Spake Zarathustra.*

9. C.S. Lewis, *The Problem of Pain* (New York: HarperCollins, 1940), p. 121.

10. Ellen G. White, *The Desire of Ages* (Mountain View, CA: Pacific Press Publishing Association, 1940), p. 58.

11. *Ibid.*

12. While all stand guilty of the death of the "Lamb of God" who died for "the sin of the *world*," the lost show by their actions that they do not acknowledge their accountability (John 1:29, emphasis supplied); instead of repenting of their natural enmity toward God, they have cultivated it until it has become the ruling motive of their lives.

13. See Revelation 2:11; 20:6; and especially 20:14; 21:8.

14. Clark H. Pinnock, "The Conditional View," in *Four Views on Hell*, editor William Crockett (Grand Rapids, MI: ZondervanPublishingHouse, 1996), p. 145.

15. Lewis, pp. 126, 127, emphasis supplied.

16. This is why some, although lost, will not be resurrected to face their life's record. While they did not make the choices that would enable them to be entrusted with eternal life, if they are judged cognitively or emotionally incapable, they will not be held accountable for their actions. God is fair.

17. According to Strong's Concordance, entry 2654, the Greek word for "consume" in Hebrews 12:29 is *katanalisko*, which means "to consume *utterly*," emphasis supplied.

18. See Matthew 8:12; 22:13; 25:30.

19. Lewis, p. 130, emphasis supplied.

20. Jay Adams, *The Grand Demonstration* (Santa Barbara, CA: EastGate Publishers, 1991), p. 113.

21. Pinnock, p. 148. The dualistic belief in the natural immortality of the soul is a Hellenistic contrivance. As mentioned in Chapter Four, endnote 7, see Edward William Fudge, *The Fire That Consumes: The Biblical Case for Conditional Immortality* (Carlisle, UK: The Paternoster Press, 1994) for an exhaustive study of the subject.

Chapter Eighteen

Into His Marvelous Light

The fires that consumed the wicked have purified the earth. Like a newborn in freshness and vigor, the planet that had been the battlefield of the great controversy between good and evil comes forth in restored innocence. The millions of saved have been transported from heaven to the new earth, where they will live out their endless days in a world purged of sin. The tree of life brings forth its fruit, wreathed in healing leaves. Virginal streams undulate by tree-lined banks. Meadows lead to plains, which swell into grand mountains that meet a purified sky. Microscopic minutia and grand panorama alike manifest perfection and harmony. The most detailed inspection as well as the widest pan of the cosmos reveals no trace of sin. The only evidence of its existence is found in the marks of crucifixion in the head, hands, feet and side of Jesus. Those wounds, once gaping wide in pain, are now an indelible reminder of the love that conquered death.

The jeweled gates and golden walls of the New Jerusalem radiate brighter than the sun, for God Himself is the light source. Yet there is nothing about this light that assaults the senses. The inhabitants hold face-to-face communion with their God, and know Him even as they are known. Free of sin, they can stand in His direct presence, looking into His holy eyes, and feel only comfort and joy.

A child prances into vibrant green grass before the holy temple. From the throne comes a light that is dazzling, yet welcome to her eyes. As she jumps and laughs in ecstasy, the form of her Savior approaches, hands held out as if asking for a dance. In His eyes she sees an infinite knowing, an awareness that penetrates the depths of her soul. She does not turn away from His comprehending gaze, or squint at the sheer brilliance of His face. She beholds with unshaded eye the source of infinite love.

Visit us online at **www.amazingfacts.org** and
check out our online catalog filled with other great
books, videos, CDs, audiotapes, and more!

Or call **1-800-538-7275**

Don't miss our FREE online
Bible Prophecy course at **www.bibleuniverse.com**
Enroll today and expand your universe!